THE TREMENDUM

THE
TREMENDUM.

A THEOLOGICAL
INTERPRETATION
OF THE HOLOCAUST

ARTHUR A. COHEN

CROSSROAD • NEW YORK

1981
The Crossroad Publishing Company
18 East 41st Street, New York, NY 10017

Printed in the United States of America

Library of Congress Cataloging in Publication Data

Cohen, Arthur Allen, 1928–
    The tremendum.

    1. Holocaust (Jewish theology)   I. Title.
BM645.H6C63   296.3'87   81–52
ISBN 0–8245–0006–7

CONTENTS

FOREWORD

To read Arthur A. Cohen's *The Tremendum: A Theological Interpretation of the Holocaust* is to believe anew in the necessity of theology. So accustomed can we become to the debasement of both the secular and the theological currencies that we can be startled in the face of the rarest of human achievements: genuinely theological thinking. The reader of this singular work will find here thinking on its ownmost ground.

To think the *tremendum* is to think an actuality of our history that, as Arthur Cohen shows, cannot—yet must—be thought. To think theologically in this situation means to demand new "thought-full" language. That newness may sometimes prove to be an old language radically revised because genuinely rethought. So it is here in Cohen's revisionary retrieval of Rudolph Otto's language for the holy as the uncanny *mysterium tremendum:* that fascinating and frightening mystery that transcends all thought and history. As Cohen rethinks Otto, an unnerving sea-change occurs for both our religious experience and our theology. For Otto's "transcending" *mysterium tremendum* is deconstructed and rethought into Cohen's "subscending" *tremendum*. To think the Holocaust as the *tremendum* of the overwhelming power of a radical evil that subscends thought and action alike is to force theologians to think again. To think, with Cohen, of the caesura erupting in all the traditions through the power of the *tremendum* is to dare to think a tradition through again. Through that caesura we must undertake a deconstructive journey which our more usual, domesticated language of "rupture" or "break" no longer yields.

This demand for new theological language like the language of *"tremendum"* and "caesura" empowers Cohen's initial reflections.

Through such "thought-full" language Cohen helps us resist the
kind of "thought-less-ness" which, as Hannah Arendt insisted, in-
flicts our doxic, language-ridden moment. Surely both Arendt and
Cohen are correct here. We cannot think theologically about the
Holocaust if we simply continue to use the exhausted languages of
the traditions. Even the expression "radical evil" cannot provoke
the demand for thought that the unsettling, unexpected phrase
"the *tremendum*" will. To declare that a rupture or a radical break
has occurred in our culture and our thought can tempt us to a sense
of déjà vu, evoking a thoughtlessness which the deconstructive
word "caesura" resists.

As our language collapses in upon itself to disclose the banaliza-
tion of existence, our concepts can become mere categories, our
best theological paradoxes mere *doxai*. We begin to sense the need
for both language and thought to be deconstructed before constructive theology can occur again. Only then might we be freed to
think again. For the theologian, this pervasive sense of an
exhausted language geared to thoughtlessness intensifies to an anxiety that all may be lost. For theology is nothing if it cannot think.
Theology is spent if it cannot think the limit-concept of all our
thought—the limit-concept empowering what should be the ultimate limit-word, "God." What happens in a thoughtless situation
to thinkers committed to *logos* on *theos*, to theo-logy? What indeed?
What word in our language now seems more banalized, less disclosive, less frightening or gracious than the one limit-word that be-
speaks the single reality theology dares to think—the uncanny,
dangerous word "God." And what intellectual enterprise within
traditional theology can seem more one-dimensional, more beside
the point in the age of the *tremendum*, than traditional theodicies?
These theodicies were once noble expressions of the risk of genuine
thought. Now they appear as Piranesi-like ruins exposing the shattered fragments of the words "God" and "evil" alike.

Arthur Cohen's instincts for the heart of the contemporary
theological dilemma are profoundly right. Only a new and defamiliarizing and deconstructive language, one forged in the process of thought upon those linked incommensurable realities, the
tremendum and God, can free us to think again. Only a language
impelled by the caesura from within, a language expressive of the
abyss in our culture (both secular and religious), the caesura in our
domesticated religious thoughts and our battered liturgies, can
free theological thought to speak again.

It is history itself—our history, that history which smashed against itself in the Holocaust—that has exposed the pathos of earlier liberal theologies. Those earlier liberal theologies were courageous and disclosive expressions of enlightenment and emancipation. But to repeat them now is to issue the theological equivalent of a Hallmark card of condolence—well-intentioned, tired, sad, pathetic. Even the more recent Jewish and Christian neo-orthodox theologies—those splendid and liberating expressionist outbursts of paradox, ambiguity, and negation impelled by a sense of the radical verticality of divine transcendence—have now crashed upon the inverse verticality, the subscension of individual historicity by the sheer force of the *tremendum* of the Holocaust as global history.

As the reader of this daring book soon discovers, we can find no easy way out of our uncanny dilemma. Cohen will force us to feel and, through that feeling, to think the *tremendum*. He will honor earlier liberal and neo-orthodox theologies (including his own earlier work) in the only honorable way left to those who confront the *tremendum*. He will deconstruct their innocence, expose their illusions, and retrieve their intent to think. He will insist that the great heritage of Jewish orthopraxis and Jewish theology must be accorded the most committed hermeneutical reflection even now. He will commit himself to rethink and retrieve the classic Jewish responses to earlier catastrophes and survivals of the Jewish people: the rabbinic tradition's response to the destruction of the Temple and the beginning of the long exile, the kabbalists' response to the expulsion of Spanish Jewry. He will honor his great predecessors as the classic thinkers they are: Philo, Maimonides, Halevi, Mendelssohn, Buber, and, above all, Rosenzweig. He will pay heed to the reflections of his contemporaries: the Mishnaic research of Jacob Neusner; the post-Holocaust reflections of Elie Weisel, Emil Fackenheim, Irving Greenberg, and others; the extraordinary recovery of the kabbalistic tradition by Gershom Scholem. Above all, as the final chapter clarifies, Cohen will insist upon speaking to and from the heart of all properly Jewish theology—the reality of the Jewish people to whose praxis and thought he holds himself and his thought finally accountable.

Like all genuine thought, Arthur Cohen's theology is grounded in a historicity that is both the history of a people and the retrieval of a heritage of classic religious thought and praxis. To think theologically in a post-Holocaust situation is to live and think historically.

Yet now, as this book makes clear, to think historically cannot become the kind of easy exercise in "historical consciousness" long since exposed by Nietzsche as a failure to think. To think historically is also to evaluate. To think historically is to develop a hermeneutics of suspicion focussed upon the illusions and the not-so-innocent theories of both ourselves and our predecessors. Only through such radical suspicion is retrieval of any tradition possible. The chapter devoted to historical theology is, therefore, fully as much a part of the constructive theological argument of the work as a whole as is the phenomenology of the *tremendum* in chapter 2 and the constructive reflection on God in chapter 4. As Hans-Georg Gadamer correctly insists, "To understand [the past] at all is to understand [it] differently." Historical theology is not a "history" of theological opinions. Historical theology is theology. It is thinking. It is "thought-full" conversation with the classics on the fundamental questions on the meaning of our existence before God. Those same questions have found responses in the classic texts, images, symbols, events, persons, rituals, and thoughts of every classic religious tradition. If those questions are to be asked anew and those responses are to be retrieved as thought, not merely repeated as opinion, they must be understood differently. Otherwise they will not be understood at all.

To understand any tradition after the *tremendum* is to retrieve its genius through a retrieval that is also a suspicion. Through that kind of hermeneutics, we may find hidden, forgotten, even repressed aspects of the tradition for thought now. A hermeneutical enterprise like this occurs in the powerful theological reflections of the final chapter of this work. There the reader will find Arthur Cohen's own constructive rethinking of the reality of God in a post-*tremendum* age. Unless I misread him, Arthur Cohen moves in this section through a powerful hermeneutics of suspicion to an equally powerful hermeneutics of retrieval. By that dangerous route he retrieves for thought the deconstructive mode of thinking of the Jewish kabbalistic tradition historically retrieved by Scholem, the negative theology in the gnostic-kabbalistic tradition from Boehme through Schelling, and, above all, the unthought that must now be thought in the mystic epistemology and ontology of the incomparable Franz Rosenzweig.

Cohen does not allow himself simply to "repeat" the solutions of his chosen classics, those defamiliarizing trajectories of the tradition. The choice of these particular classics is both liberating and courageous. For precisely these classic modes of deconstructive thought, let us recall, were and are still often despised when not altogether forgotten or repressed by both Jewish and Christian theologians in favor of some "clearer" or "more orthodox" aspect of the traditions. As Cohen's creative rethinking of the position of Franz Rosenzweig makes especially clear, he understands this sub-terranean tradition of negative deconstructive theological reflec-tion on God only by understanding it differently. He must so un-derstand it for Cohen understands it post-*tremendum*. Traditional deconstruction must itself now be deconstructed in order to be retrieved at all. By this complex and daring strategy, Cohen aids us all to break through the thoughtlessness of so much contemporary theology, both Jewish and Christian. He demands a rethinking of the most difficult, complex, unnerving, and uncanny traditions in all Western theological reflection on God—traditions of thought where the radically negative is intrinsic to all self-deconstructing thought in theology and may well be internal to the reality of God's own self.

By forcing this constructive retrieval upon the attention of con-temporary theology, Cohen unsettles our more usual options. Even those contemporary theodicies which most share Cohen's own clearly "bipolar" vision of God's reality (like process theodocies) now also stand accused of not facing in thought the radical power of evil disclosed for all to see in the *tremendum*.

Arthur Cohen is also respectful toward but unsatisfied with the more familiar options for serious post-Holocaust thought in con-temporary Jewish religious thought. He respects but will not ac-cept either the "eclipse of God" of Martin Buber or the "death of God" of Richard Rubenstein. As one who both insists upon narra-tive in thought and has made his mark as one of our foremost novelists, Cohen clearly honors the turn to narrative-as-thought. But he does not share Elie Wiesel's hesitancy to move through narrative to explicitly conceptual theological thought. Cohen's move to retrieve Rosenzweig and Schelling distances his position as well from the brilliant Hegelian post-Holocaust reflections of Emil Fackenheim. Just as surely Cohen's lack of emphasis on re-trieving the complex covenant traditions in the history of Jewish thought distinguishes his position from Irving Greenberg's radi-cally revisionary post-Holocaust covenant theology.

As a Christian theologian, I cannot presume to comment further on this profoundly inner-Jewish theological discussion. This much,

however, I will presume to say. I have become convinced that contemporary Jewish theologians are thinking for and in their tradition, to be sure; yet they are also thinking on behalf of all theologians in all traditions as they risk deconstruction and rethinking of
the actuality of our relationship to God in a post-*tremendum* age.
The seriousness and richness of the kind of thought already present
in contemporary Jewish theology is now intensified by the original
proposals of this work: a work by means of which Arthur Cohen
honors the entire theological community. To force us all to face and
feel the Holocaust, to demand that we dare to think in the presence
of that abyss of unspeakable evil, to unmask our temptations to
thoughtlessness by forging new language for thought—the *tremendum*, the caesura, the negative, deconstructive mystical epistemology and ontology in the actuality of all thought on God that is
faithful to the disclosure and concealment of God's reality in our
day—to risk this enterprise, I repeat, is to accomplish a task of
genuine theological thinking which every thoughtful theologian
will honor by engaging critically and every thoughtless one had
best now find more clever ways to try to evade.

One final word. I write as a Christian theologian. As such, a few
reflections to the Christian readers of this work may perhaps be in
order. My first question must be a blunt one: Why do so many
Christian theologians still refuse to face the *tremendum* which the
Holocaust discloses? (I include most of my own work in this in-
dictment.) When the reason is, as it often is, that the Christian
sense of repentance and guilt for the revolting history of Christian
anti-Semitism is the cause for Christian theological silence, the
option can be respected. And yet guilt and repentance and the
genuine religious praxis empowering both cannot become the occasion to avoid thought. Silence is possible, as silence, only to a
speaker. Theology lives or dies as serious thinking on God and all
things, including ourselves, in relationship to that God.

When even those Christian theologians most committed to thinking in relationship to the frightening history of our age (especially
most liberation and political theologians) ignore both the
Holocaust and the history of Christian anti-Semitism, something is
profoundly awry. When the subject of the *tremendum* becomes a
subject only discussed in the context of the "Jewish-Christian
dialogue," then the subject is quietly trivialized by Christian
theologians as an inner-Christian theological challenge. No less
than for Jewish theology does the *tremendum* and the caesura de-

mand new Christian theological reflection. Our classic and our contemporary theodicies are now speechless. Our serious theological reflections on the reality of God must now occur within the uncanny realm of a recognition of the *tremendum*. The courageous, revisionary, and still largely unheeded post-Holocaust christological reflections of such Christian theologians as Gregory Baum, Roy Eckardt, Franklin Littell, Johann Baptist Metz, Jürgen Moltmann, John Pawlikowski, Rosemary Radford Ruether, and Paul van Buren should be listened to and seriously reflected upon by all Christian theologians. And yet even these revisionary christological proposals cannot be enough. For, as this work of Arthur Cohen makes clear, even the best revisionary theological reflections on the central symbols of each tradition (the covenant symbol for many Jewish theologians; the Christ symbol for many Christian theologians) must finally yield to the kind of thought that constitutes all properly theological reflection: thought on the reality of God.

Only when Christian theologians join their Jewish theological colleagues to think the reality of God post-*tremendum* will a genuine dialogue really begin. Only then will the thoughtlessness that threatens to engulf us all cease. The critical response of the entire theological community—Jewish and Christian—to this extraordinarily thoughtful work of Arthur Cohen will prove a singularly good test of whether theology does indeed dare to think.

DAVID TRACY
The University of Chicago

PREFACE

The four chapters which constitute this volume were originally developed as public lectures, the first delivered as the
Leo Baeck Memorial Lecture for 1974 and published by the
Leo Baeck Institute under the title "Thinking the Tremendum: Some Theological Implications of the Death Camps,"
and the three that follow as the Tisch Lectures in Judaic
Theology sponsored by the Department of Religion at
Brown University in 1979. All of the lectures have been con-
siderably revised and modified for publication, although the
underlying argument of each remains unaltered.

The Tisch Lectures were construed by their Brown University Department of Religion sponsors as a demonstration
exercise in the viability of teaching Jewish theology in a
university environment. I am confident my lectures did not
persuade them; moreover, their interest and my own could
not have been farther apart. Not unusually the teaching of
Jewish studies cannot maintain the distinction between reviewing the history of Jewish thought (which I call "historical theology") and thinking theologically. It is a distinction
which seems transparent if one is involved, for instance, in
philosophy, since obviously the philosopher teaching the
history of philosophy is doing something different from setting forth his own philosophic critique and describing the
contemporary philosophic agenda. The reason why it is so

difficult for departments of religion and, more particularly, programs of Jewish studies to maintain such a distinction is that the academic faculty engaged in Jewish studies is far less qualified to profess theology than is a philosopher to philosophize. Most teachers of Jewish studies are trained as Jewish historians, which means that they know Jewish materials but are not necessarily concerned with issues of Jewish belief. Of course, it is often maintained that issues of Jewish belief are irrelevant to Jewish life and endurance, the emphatic weight falling upon matters of Jewish ethnicity or unreflectively upon the detail of Jewish observance, without any regard to the content and form of Jewish belief. An extended critique of such a misinformed and naive conception as this would take me far afield, but the demurral expressed above does explain something of my refusal to adopt certain conventional procedures in these chapters. I am not interested, for instance, in reviewing the positions of others, except as dialectical foils to my own. Moreover, I am interested in developing a theological language out of the calamity of Jewish historical existence which is not only relevant to the Jew but to any other monotheist.

Among the very few pleasures of my Brown experience was my meeting with David Tracy, Langdon Gilkey, and Ray Hart whom I now count among my friends. I was pleased as well by the opportunity afforded me of reacquainting myself with Richard Rubinstein from whose thought I still find myself estranged but of whose profundity and seriousness I have no doubt. At various times, conversation and the exchange of ideas with David Stern, William Green, David Biale, and Art Green have proved very stimulating and valuable to me, and I thank them for their response.

My particular gratitude goes to David Tracy for his willingness to write a foreword to this volume. His own command of theological method and conception, profound as these are, is nothing to me when set alongside his passion for theology. David Tracy makes vivid and significant for me the obligation—which I for one am so often willing to put aside—to think theologically. He renews for me the importance to God of being understood better.

ARTHUR A. COHEN

· 1 ·

THINKING THE TREMENDUM

There is something in the nature of thought—its patient de-
liberateness and care for logical order—that is alien to the
enormity of the death camps. There is something no less in
the reality of the death camps that denies the attentions of
thought. Thinking and the death camps are incommensurable. The procedures of thought and the ways of knowing are
confounded. It is to think the unthinkable—an enterprise
that is not alone contradictory but hopeless—for thought
entails as much a moral hope (that it may be triumphant,
mastering its object, dissolving the difficulties, containing
and elucidating the conundrum) as it is the investment of
skill and dispassion in a methodic procedure.

The death camps are a reality which, by their very nature,
obliterate thought and the humane program of thinking. We
are dealing, at the very outset, therefore, with something
unmanageable and obdurate—a reality which exists, which
is historically documented, which has specific beginnings
and ends, located in time, the juncture of confluent influ-
ences which run from the beginnings of historical memory
to a moment of consummating orgy, never to be forgotten,
but painful to remember, a continuous scourge to memory
and the future of memory and yet something which,
whenever addressed, collapses into tears, passion, rage. The
death camps are unthinkable, but not unfelt. They consti-

1

tute a traumatic event and, like all decisive trauma, they are suppressed but omnipresent, unrecognized but tyrannic, silted over by forgetfulness but never obliterated.

Thirty-five years have passed since the closing of the death camps. The first decade after the revelation of the murder of the Jews was passed in defining the language of formal description and formal judgment. It was the time of the statistical accounting, the development of an accurate historical language, the numbering of the victims, the definition of the grammar of genocide, and the no less walleyed, benumbed dealing of judgment to the accused, culminating in the Eichmann trial of 1961. The second period saw the rescue of a literature, the beginnings of the controversies of interpretation, the publication of fictional accounts of the camps and autobiographic documents, by the quick and the dead, from Chaim Kaplan, Emmanuel Ringelbaum, Ilse Aichinger, Michel Tournier, Andre Schwarzbart, J. P. Steiner, Elie Wiesel, Pyotr Rawicz, to mention a few among countless others. The task of this literature was neither to astonish nor to amaze, neither to exalt nor to humiliate, but to provide a vivifying witness to the flesh of the dead and the mortal objectivity of the statistics.

It is during the third decade and out of the fourth that a new moment in the assimilation of the historical reality began. Another generation, those who knew not, had grown up—a generation that knows the birth and struggle of the State of Israel but knows nothing directly of the Hitler years and the immediate shock of their ferocity. To this generation the question of meaning has become critical. It is the generation that bears the scar without the wound, sustaining memory without direct experience. It is this generation that has the obligation, self-imposed and self-accepted (however ineluctably), to describe a meaning and wrest instruction from the historical, while believing (perhaps innocently) that understanding is shield and buckler against repetition of the same catastrophe. To achieve this prophylactic sense, this preventive vision, is the task not alone of energizing memory, hearing the witnesses, attending to their words and warnings, but of thought as well. It is not enough to deal with the reality of the death camps viscerally, with passion and anguish, with guilt for surviving and abashment before the enormity, with rage and anger, sublimated, as Jewish anger has always been. These are not enough, nor are they even sufficient. It is simply not adequate to *feel* this enormous event. One must live with it, and living with it requires that it be perceived accurately (to the extent that accuracy is possible about events as charged as these), clearly (to the extent that looking into the charnel house can ever be cool observation), and distinctly (to the extent that it can be identified in its uniqueness, despite all its resemblances to other crimes of history).

There was a time when it was understandable that one's reaction to the asking of the meaning of this event was the fervid wish that it had none, that it implicated nothing beyond itself, that it described an historical horror, but that it did not tear apart the fabric of the larger universe where human beings create, make art, think, love, ransoming the human from the mud and muck of the concrete and particular. That time is past.

The question of meaning is asked both immodestly and modestly, depending as one's rage and vulnerability thwarts the project of thought by denying to *the event* its community with the reasonable (that it has cause, antecedent, precursor, and therefore might be forecast and predicted), and hence its negative meaning (that the history of all peoples is marked by episodes of transcending brutality and cruelty). But clearly thinking the *enormous event* is one thing, comprehending it and expressing its meaning quite another. Obviously, the difficulty derives from the fact that the meaning of *the event* is different from the meaning of a word or a simple description. The moral valence implicit in the conception of any meaning at all creates the difficulty. The meaning of a declarative proposition ("this is") or a defining disclosure ("the sun is a . . .") adds to the coherence of the universe of speech by making our language more precise and significant. It is moral in the limited sense that linguistic meaning is generally regarded as a contribution to the clarity of conceptions from which our sense of things proceeds. Order, clarity, coherence are values which undergird the moral authority of meaning.

The meaning of an historical event is different than the meaning of a propositional assertion. History never means one thing; its judgments are always ambiguous, because the past is never fully available. Even where our judgments are unequivocal (and assertions of meaning are judgments), the act of judging is already a movement of the mind beyond the evidence to a reckoning, a totaling, a summation. And what would it matter if we pass judgment upon *the event* in the conventional language of good and evil? The judgment of good and evil seems pallid and worn-out; the language of theodicy weary and insignificant. How can we mean much with "good and evil"?

One of the intentions of moral judgment is admonitory and preventive. It is our betrayed hope that when we call an event evil, we record the verdict to caution the future. Clearly unavailing, the historical future is not warned. The meaning of the past—its moral valence—neither warns nor does it prevent. The search for meaning has, therefore, no pragmatic efficacy. Its only value is that it may oblige us to remedy the machinery of conceptions in which moral expectation and moral credibility still hold sway—irrational sway, but sway nonetheless.

The issue of meaning is raised not because I am persuaded *the event* has a meaning (for it offers no guidance or instruction), but rather because I am persuaded it has no meaning, because it denies meaning and makes mockery of meaning. And yet a whole way of regarding the universe—the Jewish and Christian monopolar divinity of absolutes and superiorities—rests upon a universe where all meanings lead to Him Who Is, the God of meaning, who bestows meaning and secures the sovereignty of meaning. The God of meaning is either not the God of ancient meaning (in this sense only is he dead) or he must be a newly understood God because, clearly, he and we deal in this century with a meaningless enormity that decisively concludes that age of past illusion where meaning was judgment and hope.

I

We are in the fourth decade. The distance between ourselves and *the event* of the *tremendum* has grown. The survivors persist, most in private communication with their memories, most silent; others, vigorously, often desperately trying to bridge the chasm which opened beneath them, then, nearly forty years ago, talking to us well and badly, convincingly and shrilly, patiently and irritably, superior to us and supercilious, guarding as they do a body of images and imaginings; or else vaguely and mystically, floating beyond us, palpable ghosts and spectres of a world we never knew. To the side of the survivors have come, however, in recent years, other aides and interpreters, the thinkers.

It is as someone who is trying to think about the *tremendum* of the event that I write. My preliminary observations fall into two general and primary categories: thinking about the historical and thinking about the meaning of the historical.

The predicament one faces at the very outset is that the procedures of traditional historical thought afford us very little assistance. Historiography is a patient accumulation of relevant information with a view to describing and interpreting events. The Dutch historian, Pieter Geyl, made it abundantly clear in his ongoing argument with Leopold von Ranke that history may be value-free, but that historiography is never. Writing history is not simply telling what happened. The historian always tells what happened from the historian's point of view. Geyl, writing of Napoleon while detained by the Nazis in a privileged concentration camp, showed how European historians of Napoleon and of the Napoleonic era—Taine, Quinet, Sorel, and others—constructed a Napoleon who was true to some facts, but not to all; accurate to part of the reality, but not to the whole; and in the process, a liberal Napoleon, a reactionary Napoleon, a bourgeois Napoleon, a middle-class or an elitist Napoleon rose and fell. The facts were all there, but historians select. When a work of history refuses to select, when it has no point of view, it cannot construe history. Instead, it retires into chronicle and accumulation, telling all and obfuscating everything.

Historiography must always select and combine, reconstruct and pattern, establish causalities and coincidences. One judges the acuteness and probability of truth by the ability of the historian to contain more of the reality, to reconcile its living contrariety and dissolve its palpable confusion, rather than by whether the story it tells is what one has all along believed or wants to believe. Great historical writing renovates familiar readings of history and, however *parti pris*, whatever its loyalties to one or another ideological movement or doctrinaire position, it reveals its dependence upon a structure of value.

Traditional historiography does not help our dealing with the *tremendum* of the genocide of European Jewry precisely because the reality exceeds its causalities. Nothing before, not the French Revolution, not the unification of Germany, not the emancipation of the Jews, not the rise of capitalism, not the teaching of contempt according to the Gospels and Church Fathers, none of these—causalities though they may be—achieves more than a gloss of the enormity—explicating this or that aspect of the Nazi movement, interpreting this or that current of mob psychology or popular ideology, but leaving intact and unexplained the singularity of a machinery conceived and constructed to destroy a whole people.

If not historiography as a satisfactory tool, are there not other disciplines of inquiry, the investigation of the psychological and linguistic conceits of the perpetrators and their victims which will assist us? Is it not relevant to understand the modes of deviance which released the psyche and language of a civilized society from the bonds of morality to the development of which its own traditions of *Kultur* had so profoundly contributed? What allowed, such a course of inquiry might investigate, the degeneration of German speech, over the length of a half-century, from the rich, imbricated, responsible pursuit of truth into the garbled, vulgarized German authorized and distributed by the Nazi press, Nazi literature, and official bureaucratic speech.

Such an inquiry would be illuminating, but ultimately ineffectual, since the debasement of language and the traducing of the psyche, dependent as it is upon the organ of speech, is a process observable in varying degrees in all Western language. The case of the German language is only an example of more so, but there is little doubt that the same may be observed in Soviet Russia, and one notes in advanced capitalist societies that the command of nuanced and subtle language in public discourse has all but disappeared. The debasement of language, the stripping of its shading and moral intensity began in the West long before Hitler and continues after he is gone. It will help us to explain a kind of cauterization of conscience by the use of metaphor and euphemism; to understand that in official Nazi language the extermination of Jews was precisely that—the disinfectant of lice, the burning of garbage, the incineration of trash, and hence language never had to say

exactly what acts its words commanded: kill, burn, murder
that old Jew, that middle-aged Jew, that child Jew. Language created its own rhetoric of dissimulation, and conscience was no longer required to hear accurately—a phenomenon not unique in Nazi Germany, but, indisputably, a
consequential aspect of its discipline.

II

Whatever we may learn from history, moral philosophy,
psychopathology, or political science about the conditions
which preceded and promoted the death camps, or the behavior of oppressors and victims which obtained within the
death camps, is unavailing. All analysis holds us within the
normative kingdom of reason, and however the palpable irrationality of the events, the employment of rational
analysis is inappropriate. I do not feel the calm of reason to
be obscene as some critics of the rational inquiry into the
tremendum have described it. It is not obscene for human
beings to try to retain their sanity before an event which
disorders sanity. It is a decent and plausible undertaking. It
is simply inappropriate and unavailing. Probative inquiry
and dispassionate reason have no place in the consideration
of the death camps, precisely because reason possesses a
moral vector. To reason, that is to estimate and evaluate,
is to employ discernment and discrimination before a
moral ambiguity. The *tremendum* is beyond the discourse
of morality and rational condemnation. It is not that the
death camps were absolutely evil. Such judgments do not
help. It is not enough to pronounce them absolutely evil.
Absolute evil is a paradigm. There is nothing to which we
can point in the history of men and nations which is absolutely evil, although the criterion of that abstraction has
helped moralists to pronounce upon the relative evils of
history.

Absolute evil—even if it designated something real—

would be an inept formulation, for what does it mean, in fact, to say of some thing or event that it is absolutely evil? It means only that we can conceive of no greater evil, whereas in truth we can: we can conceive of a system that can murder all life (assuming, of course, that abundant life is an absolute good), but clearly this adds nothing to our absolute but exaggeration. We look for qualitative enrichment of our moral sensibility, a texturing and refinement, while all our language before the event presses us to grosser and more extreme formulations.

The relativity of evil in the deliberations of moralists rarely entails the exposition of the relative good. Relative evils do not complete themselves by the description of relative goods. Relative evil is measured in the mind against absolute evil. Of course, such a logic of moral experience has an ultimate reckoning. If it is commonplace for human beings to free themselves from the paradigm of the absolute, it becomes ever easier to ignore or to excuse transgression. Human beings learn to rationalize and justify so artfully and so well that the right time passes unobserved, when they should have shouted "no, not this, not this." But, of course, it is hard in a shouting and busy world, continuously assaulted by interests and needs, for any single human being to be heard warning against evil. During such times, the recognition that there are indeed absolute evils (even though abstractly described) has not prevented us from accumulating a mountain of small evils which, like the bricks of the Tower of Babel, might one day reach up and pierce the heavens. The point of this is to suggest that moral convention, a pragmatic regimen of norms and *regulae* of behavior retain their authority only so long as the absolute evil of which they are special and modest *exempla* remains abstract and unrealized. When absolute evil ceases, however, to be the abstract warning of the impending and possible and comes to be, how shall the descriptive domains of the moral and immoral retain their authority? Can one doubt the relevance of this to the politics of the twentieth century? Until the end of the eighteenth century the political theory of Europe centered about philosophies of law, right, duty, and freedom. It was understood that the relation of citizen and state was somehow a moral relation, that the citizen was a person educated to freedoms and informed by responsibilities. In our time such language has virtually disappeared from public inquiry and debate. The language of politics is not that of moral interaction and representation, but the calibration and weighting of power, influence, need, control in such fashion as to guarantee for one's own constituency a larger and measurably greater security both for and against uncontested aggression. Questions of right and law, of justice and equity have virtually disappeared as moral criteria for social and political action. The consequence of all this— the process of the demoralization of the political—is the consequent irrelevance of the "absolute" and the "utter" as the adjectival thunder of the putatively relative. What civilization once called murder or barbarism or cruelty or sadism has in our day become a useless rhetoric. Not one of us can summon these words with the authority with which John Milton or Voltaire might have spoken them, and few can hear the English rendering of the Hebrew prophets with little more than a recognition of their immense eloquence. Words no longer command us, precisely because they no longer reflect concepts and convictions which directly govern and thereby agitate conscience.

If this analysis is correct, it will be readily understood why I have come to regard the death camps as a new event, one severed from connection with the traditional presuppositions of history, psychology, politics, and morality. Anything which we might have known before the *tremendum* of this event is rendered conditional by its utterness and extremity. Note that I have not referred to Auschwitz as the name by which to concretize and transmit the reality of the *tremendum*. Auschwitz was only one among many sites of death. It was not even the largest death camp, although it may well have claimed the largest number of victims. Auschwitz is a particularity, a name, a specific. Auschwitz is the German name for a Polish name. It is a name which belongs to *them*. It is not a name which commemorates. It is both specific and other. And, if my perception is correct, what occurred then, from the time of the conception of the "Final Solution" until the time that surreal "idealism" was interrupted, is the transmutation of chosen persons into chosen people, of the scandal of Jewish particularity and doggedness into the scandal of Jewish universality. What might have been, until the time of the Final Solution, a controversy about the particularism and insularity of Judaism in contradistinction to the dogma of nationalist anti-Semites who wanted a Jewry divested of Judaism and Jewish identity, or a Jewish theological reform which wanted Jews rehabilitated by Western humanism and *Kultur*, or a Zionism which wanted Jews tied both to self-determination and socialist class consciousness in the struggle against Jewish temerity and timorousness, became in the death camps the brute factuality of the universal. Not the individual Jew, not the martyred Jew, not the survived Jew—not a Jew by any name or fortune—not such a Jew of particularity was chosen. Jew, simple Jew, nominative universal describing and containing all mankind that bears that racial lineament until the third generation of ancestry, became chosen and was universalized. The death camps ended forever one argument of history—whether the Jews are a chosen people. They are chosen, unmistakably, extremely, utterly.

III

The uniqueness of the death camps, that which makes them a novelty *in extremis*, severed from all normative connections to historical precedent and causality, imparts to them a phenomenological simplicity. The death camps are a reality quite literally *sui generis*. Insofar as their reality is concerned, it is not necessary for us to perform phenomenological surgery, to bracket them, to excise their connections from the welter of historical conditions, to clarify the standpoint of perception in order not to confuse their manifestation with that of any other seemingly comparable phenomenon, like the social institution of the prison or the army. Simply defined (and the simpler the better for our purposes), the death camps were constructed to fulfill one purpose: to kill the greatest number of Jews at the least possible cost in money and material. To the side of Jews were added Gypsies, another "degenerative and infectious race," and the work was undertaken and, by war's end, almost completed. It was a task pursued with lethal self-sacrifice since, quite clearly, as many historians have noted, the war effort of the German army was severely impaired by the preference given to the transport of Jews. The simplicity of the phenomenon is no less its enormity. To kill Jews, any and all, defines the reality and clarifies its uniqueness. In the long history of "the teaching of contempt," in Jules Isaac's telling epitomization of the Christian doctrine of the rejection and humiliation of the Jewish people, the Church never undertook to kill the Jews. Certainly, the Church had the opportunity; it did not have the intent. As Professor Yosef Hayim Yerushalmi has pointed out, the anti-Jewish massacres of medieval times were "principally the work of the mob and the rabble" and, as he elaborates elsewhere in the same remarks, were often interrupted and contained by the appeals of cardinals and popes, rather than being the consequence of their instigation. This is not to say that Jews and

Judaism were beloved to the Church. It is merely to indicate what should not be forgotten, that the practice of the Church was as ambivalent toward the Jews as was its theology. It acknowledged that Judaism was a *religio licita*, a legally permissible religion, even though a deluded one; that it worshiped the true God, although inadequately; that it was a primary faith, although one humiliated and superseded. The most telling observation of Yerushalmi in this context is his ironic suggestion that had the Church not rejected the Marcionite heresy which specified the distinct and unrelated dualism of the God of creation (that of Hebrew scriptures) and the God of redemption (the Jesus of the Gospels), the Jews might well have been destroyed. Precisely because the Church did not disdain its origins, did not repudiate the God of Israel, the Jews survived. Indeed, the novelty of the death camps is further underscored. The medieval tradition of anti-Semitism was *contra Judaeos*, against the faith and the belief of the Jews, and, only by inference, against the people and the ethnicity that sustained that faith. The older traditions of anti-Semitism, those that stretch back into Roman times, the rage of Apion and Manetho, the confusions of Tacitus and others, signify an uncritical perception of the Jews as a political unit, a religious commonwealth that refused Rome, not allegiance, but moral capitulation. The ancient Jews annoyed Rome less because they were different, than because they regarded those respects in which they differed—notably theology—to be superior to Rome. Perhaps there, well before Christianity, the seed-bed of racial contempt is to be found, the ultimate historical ground of Sartre's contention in *Anti-Semite and Jew* that the anti-Semite chooses to make himself nondescript, to attach himself to the solidarity of the miserable mob, to make himself mediocre precisely because he cannot make himself individual. The anti-Semite takes upon himself the vulnerability of the state, the difficulties of an abstract, national pride and whatever there is, out there, that offends against the few values that give him identity, those he calls the menace of the Jew. Of course, Sartre's analysis is undergirded by historical assumptions with which we would take issue. But what seems to me most profound in Sartre's inquiry is the perception of racism as an instrument of insulating and aggrandizing the empty man, or, as is more appropriate to the anti-Semitism of thinkers of undeniable weight and influence, thinkers such as Marx, Bakunin, Kautsky, to name but three revolutionary intellectuals whose anti-Semitism reached grotesque proportions—their anti-Semitism was a means of interpreting their *ressentiment*, their unreasonable contempt for the slowness, the intractability, the stubborn obduracy of the old order which refused to cave in on schedule.

State-instituted racism and racial anti-Semitism are modern phenomena, whose origins may lie in the classical tradition which knew no efficient distinction between the political manipulation of religion and the religious validation of the state. During the Middle Ages, the doctrine of the two powers, the king and the bishop, in continuous tension and embattlement, the king warring to win the loyalty and the blessings and benefices of the Church, and the Church using the weapons of popular agitation and excommunication to manipulate the powers of the king, maintained a healthy imbalance in which the Jews, *servi camerae*, bond servants to both crown and cross, were more often maintained as financial and political intermediaries to their disputes than cast into the fires of either. All this delicate tension dissolved with the victory of the secular state, the state which could conceive, administer, and propagate any viewpoint throughout its realm quickly and efficiently, employing the press, the clergy, the law, the army, and the civil service as instruments of disseminating policy. If such policy was racist, the Czars could with ease send the Black

Hundred into the streets; it could invent blood libels and try the innocent as conspirators; it could invent and disseminate the Protocols of the Elders of Zion; the army could condemn Dreyfus and hold the government ransom for his condemnation; and National Socialism could institute the program of ultimate anti-Semitism, the death camps.

IV

What must be understood is that the irrational phenomenon of racism can still be made intelligible—psychologically, socially, historically. Any Jew reading Graetz's *History of the Jews* before 1939 would, I think (seduced, as he might be by Graetz's eloquence and narrative gifts), regard his summation of the many hundreds of pogroms, massacres, riots which fill his pages as being antiphonic and unremarkable: nine Jews were slain; eleven Jews died; one hundred fifty-seven Jews were thrown into the moat and perished; four hundred eleven Jews were burned; thirty-one Jews died at the stake; one Jew died from his wounds. Indeed, the familiar litany of Jewish history until the death camps was predictable: whatever the violence, Jews died. The history of the Jews could be read as the history of Jewish dead from Ibn Verga's *Rod of Judah* until the beginning of the era of the death camps.* The fact that the numbers were compassable, variant, incidental, rising and falling, great or few, without apparent pattern or consistency enabled us to regard Jewish history as a continuous narrative of Jewish lives being paid for the principle of Jewish life. Throughout it all, it could be said that Jews died *'al kiddush ha-Shem*, in sanctification of the Name of God, as martyrs to faith, although undoubtedly there were many who were ignorant Jews, Jews without

---

* Solomon ibn Verga's *Shevet Yehuda* (*Rod of Judah*) is discussed by me in *The Natural and the Supernatural Jew: An Historical and Theological Introduction* (1962; enlarged second edition, 1979), pp. 12–17.

faith, even assimilated and converted Jews, killed no less as Jews, ennobled no less as martyrs.

The death camps changed all that as well. We are given a fixed number. We deal with a single inconceivable enormity, one figure of "six million," that has neither grown nor varied, remaining a stationary imponderable. It is no less clear that the Jews who died cannot be called martyrs. This is not to say that they are not martyrs; it is only to say that the theological implication of such a martyrdom is as catastrophic for one's conception of God as it is trivializing of one's notion of martyrdom. If the reality is inconceivable, if we cannot encompass the decision of one people to gather and destroy another, attended by the complicity and inattention of all the rest of mankind, equally inconceivable is any language of compensation or heroic transfiguration. The human beings who died are made neither more sacred nor more innocent by being called martyrs; indeed, it is the case that in martyrizing them we risk dismissing them, having given them their histrionic due. The only people who have the right to call the dead of the camps martyrs are those who believe in the sanctity of martyrs and are willing themselves to be martyrs. I know such people and I believe them when they speak of the martyrs of the camps, but I also know that very often they excise from the company of those martyrs the no less murdered Jews who were nonbelieving—Jews without *mitzvot*, even assimilated Jews, socialist Jews, Jews with changed names and non-Jewish identities. No. It will not do to call them martyrs, just yet.

I have come to the point in the discussion when the hopelessness of the inquiry seems insurmountable. I have done everything I can to make the death camps not only unique, incomparable, *sui generis*, but, more to the point, beyond the deliberations of reason, beyond the discernments of moral judgment, beyond meaning itself. It is precisely for this reason that I have used one unexplained term throughout this chapter, employing it conspicuously, but never defining it. I have spoken of the death camps—a term which encases a factual phenomenological description almost neutral in its factuality. But I have also used the term *tremendum*.

I have had several occasions in recent years to reread Rudolf Otto's magisterial essay *The Idea of the Holy (Das Heilige)*.* That essay, a late product of German idealism, an early achievement of phenomenological analysis, is turned to the investigation of our knowledge of the Holy. The Holy is not simply a cognomen for God; it is not God's other name, a name among many names, standing alongside Merciful or Judge. The Holy is the dimension of God's presence; the presentness of God is his holiness. Rudolf Otto, using the Hebrew Bible with a sovereign control and a warming love of its nuance and texture, elicits from that text revelations of the presence of God which are astonishing. Indeed, astonishment, surprise, amazement are the very terms by which Otto underscores his perception of God's nearness. God is near and present, but no less terrifying and unfathomable. It is because of this affectual welter that Otto describes God in a single phrase as the *mysterium tremendum*—the utter mystery, the enormous mystery, indeed, the terror-mystery, for *tremendum* carries with it not only the aspect of vastness, but the resonance of terror.

The phenomenology of the Holy begins with the perception of the terror-mystery of God and radiates from there, qualified and moderated and textured by the traditional modes of mercy, love, justice, until the utter God becomes the Father God of *Tatenu*, until the shattering presence becomes the still, small voice, until the terror-mystery be-

---

* Rudolf Otto, *The Idea of the Holy: An Inquiry into the Non-Rational Factor in the Idea of the Divine and Its Relation to the Rational*, trans. by John W. Harvey (London: Oxford University Press, 1923), passim.

comes a God with whom human beings can coinhabit the universe.

The terror-mystery of God, the *mysterium tremendum* of divinity has always, in the phenomenology of religion, been offset and contested by underdivinities, potencies and dominions in the universe which despise such ultimacy. The perception of the demonic coexisted with the perception of the Holy. Indeed, part of the terror-mystery of God is that his manifestation in whirlwinds and at seas, in fires and in floods was often perceived at the outset as the work of his opponent, his demiurge, his particular devil. No wonder that God, in his majesty, often appears under the aspect of his terror. The ferocity of God appears to resemble the demonic. It is no less the case if one listens, as the text unfolds its narrative, that what begins in ferocity ends in a bird with an olive branch and a rainbow. The terror-mystery of the Holy becomes the love-mystery of the Holy and the terror dissolves into grace.

This is one reading of the aspect of the Holy as *mysterium tremendum*. But, let us put the case that we of the modern age are no longer able to deal with the Holy, cannot perceive it, or authenticate its presence, but contrary and fractious, regard ourselves as alone and autonomous in the universe, unbounded by laws except as conventions of power, unhedged by moralities except as consent and convenience dictate. Is it not the case that in such a civilization all that was once permitted to the infinite power of God and denied to the finite and constrained power of men is now denied to the forgotten God and given over to the potency of infinitized man? Caution: I am not proposing in this yet another gloss to the familiar discussion of Faustian man compacted to the devil, with all its attendant critique of technology, machine-culture dehumanization. The argument here is different. It is the proposal of a counter to the *mysterium tremendum*. It is the human *tremendum*, the enormity of an infinitized man, who no longer seems to fear death or, perhaps more to the point, fears it so completely, denies death so mightly, that the only patent of his refutation and denial is to build a mountain of corpses to the divinity of the dead, to placate death by the magic of endless murder.

I call the death camps the *tremendum*, for it is the monument of a meaningless inversion of life to an orgiastic celebration of death, to a psychosexual and pathological degeneracy unparalleled and unfathomable to any person bonded to life. And of the nations and cultures of the West, is there any so totally committed to life, to the choice of life and its enlargement as a system of conduct and behavior, as that of the Jews? The Jew may well be the ideal victim because his mere persistence, his sheer endurance, his refusal to die throughout four millennia until the *tremendum*, was a celebration of the tenacity of life. Every Jew who has left Judaism for Christianity has invariably—and the literature is astonishing in its confirmation of this insistence from Paul of Tarsus to Boris Pasternak—argued that the old Jew is dead, that Judaism has no more life to speak, no more novelty to contribute, nothing vital and energetic any longer to transmit to the species. The Jew is, in such literature, construed as though dead, whereas no less clearly it is necessary to mortify Judaism in order to rationalize and excuse its abandonment. The living Jew must become the dead Jew in order that the non-Jew be saved.

Martin Buber has written in a passage often cited that there is no caesura in the history of the Jews, no midpoint, no intermediation, no gap to be filled by the Holy Spirit, no descending dove of grace, no yawning time waiting for the divine incursion. Most specifically, in this teaching, Buber was addressing the absence of penultimate messianic moments. "In our view," Buber wrote, "redemption occurs forever, and none has yet occurred. Standing, bound and shackled, in the pillory of mankind, we demonstrate with the bloody body of our people the unredeemedness of the world. For us there is no cause of Jesus; only the cause of God exists for us." Buber tried to deal with the *tremendum* on several occasions, always obliquely. He spoke of our times as the eclipse of God, times when between men and God a veil had been dropped, a veil of confusion, obstinacy, or demonism through which the Word of God could not penetrate. He believed until the end of his life that God continued to speak but that no man heard. Moreover, he continued to believe that God's speech was his action and that not hearing that speech was, in effect, to destroy the efficacy of God. God spoke and created the world; God spoke and the people convenanted themselves to his service. Six million died and God's speech was not heard. Not enough. Moving rhetoric, but unfortunately not theology, not thinking. It has to be tougher than that. It has to be more than the eclipse of God. It has to be more than the death of God. It has to be more even than Nietzsche's madman proclaiming, "we have slain him." Not enough. And we know that now.

Buber's assertion that there is no caesura in Jewish history is accurate insofar as it concerns the eschatological vision of the perfecting and redemption of history, but wrong insofar as it misses the underside of history, the corrupting caesura, the abyss rather than the heavens of the historical. For the Holy there may be no caesura, but for the unholy its name *is* caesura. The discontinuity of the abyss is precisely what insures that it is both caesura and *tremendum*. The abyss of history is in this view, also a gap in normal time, no less a gap, no less a decisive gap than would be the messianic redemption. In the time of the human *tremendum*, conventional time and intelligible causality is interrupted. In that time, if not redemption, then the demonic tears the skein of events apart and man (and perhaps God no less) is compelled to look into the abyss. The Jews, for reasons no longer curious, have looked into the abyss several times in

their long history. Tradition accounts the destruction of the
Temple and the obliteration of the Jewish settlement in ancient Palestine as one abyss. There was a caesura. The abyss
opened and the Jews closed the abyss by affirming their
guilt, denying the abyss, and taking upon themselves re-
sponsibility for the demonic. Not "beyond reason," but
"within providence" became the satisfactory explanation.
The expulsion of the Jews from Spain is accounted another.
There was a caesura. The abyss opened and the Jews closed
the abyss once again not only by reaffirming their guilt, but
more by transforming the event into an end-time of ordinary
history and the beginning-time of mystic gnosis in which
a new heaven was limned and the unseen order became
transparent to mystical understanding. The death camps
of the modern world is a third. There was another caesura
of the demonic. This time the abyss opened and one-third
of the Jewish people fell in.

V

It is not possible to respond as did the survivors of the first
abyss. We do not hold ourselves guilty. We cannot say, as an
incomparably stupid Israeli rabbi is reported to have said of
the Maalot massacre, that it occurred because the school in
which the twenty-four children were slain contained
twenty-four unkosher *mezzuzot*. Such extremity of magical
thinking is hopeless, up to and including the belief that "for
all our sins are we slain." But that was an old doctrine of
providence, simplistic, but not without counterbalance of
innumerable midrashim which saw quite clearly into the
nature of the mystery. The real point is that for our ancestors, whatever the deficiencies of their popular doctrine,
they lived in the presence of the *mysterium tremendum*, the
holy God, and knew intimately the shudder and trembling of
divine immediacy. Nor do we respond, as did the survivors
of the second abyss. The kabbalistic transfiguration of the

Spanish exile and the decimation of Sephardic Jewry represented an overwhelming and ingenious reinvestment of the
historical process with a new significance, one which was
adept at reading the sign language of events and determining an arcane and previously impenetrable language of
hope. The third abyss is read, however, neither with guilt
nor with hope. To read the event with neither guilt nor with
hope is a pitiless conclusion. It lets the event lie meaningless, unrescued, unransomed. The death camps are meaningless, but they are also instructive. This is obvious, but I
do not wish to conclude these preliminaries with a recourse
to homiletics or consolations.

For the moment I must allow the brutal summation to
emerge as it must. The death camps cannot be transcended.
There is no way of obliterating their historicity by overleap-
ing them. Quite the contrary. If there is no transcendence
beyond the abyss, the abyss must be inspected further. The
descent deeper into the abyss must take place; in a word, the
abyss must be *sub-scended*, penetrated to its perceivable
depths. The task of excavating the demonic is no metaphor.
How can we regard the atomic bomb, or Vietnam, or the
revelations of Solzhenitzyn's *Gulag*, if not as modalities of
the abyss, excavations and elaborations of the human pen-
chant to self-infinity, to the ultimate *hubris* which brings not
only Jews but all creatures to the borderlands from which
there is return for none.

It begins with the Jews and it may end with the habitable
world. There is no way of making the genocidal totality of
the death camps meaningful to the non-Jew as such, precisely because every Jew who has endured to this hour is a
survivor in fact or an accidental survivor at least, whereas
for the non-Jew the genocide of the Jews is an objective
phenomenon which, on the face of it, by its definition, appears to exclude him. The non-Jew would be slain only by
having become a Jew (as occurred to many); otherwise, the

non-Jew is able to contemplate but not share in either the fate of the victims or the perpetual unease of the survivors. This is a critical distinction which makes all effort of the Christian or the non-Jewish secular opponent of racism fail to understand what exactly the death camps mean to the Jews. For the non-Jew the death camps are still, so he imagines, a paradigm of human brutality, at least an epiphenomenon. For the Jew, however, it is historically real. The Passover Haggadah commands that every Jew consider himself as though he had gone forth in exodus from Egypt. The grammatical authority of the Haggadah makes clear that this is no metaphor, whatever our wish to make apodictic language metaphoric. The authority is clear: I was really, even if not literally, present in Egypt and really, if not literally, present at Sinai. God contemplated my virtual presence then, thirty-odd centuries ago. The fact that history could not prevision and entail my presence is irrelevant. No less is it the case that the death camps account my presence really, even if not literally: hence my obligation to hear the witnesses as though I were a witness, to be with the witness as though I were a witness. It is mandatory that this real presence of all Israel in the death camps, experiencing the *tremendum*, enter the liturgy as surely as it entered the narration of the Exodus. Within us, there is always hope and despair, and within faith that twin constellation must be honored, the hope extended by God to man and the despair returned by man to God—the dialectic most grimly enacted in our time.

Acknowledging such necessity, we must nonetheless guard against such urgency. The rush to make liturgy and midrash out of the holocaust exemplifies the tremendous internal pressure within Jewish life to seize upon *the event* as a source of potential homeostasis. This is not to say that the motive is illegitimate, only to observe that the result is guaranteed to be factitious and deceptive. Midrash, no less than liturgy, reflects centuries of distillation beyond thought. The imaginative transformation which is the accomplishment of both midrash and liturgy begins first with the transmission of the event in all its literal factuality. As the wonder and authority of the event mount through time, thought encounters it and reflects upon its complexity. Only later, in the aftermath of thought, when the terms of the event are settled and the text of its unfolding transcribed, is the imagination set free to wander through its implication. The rabbinic sources allude to debates about the nature of God, freedom, history. Those debates are briefly noted for the argument is long forgotten (or more accurately is long since incorporated in the institutions and custom of the people). We have today no such patient machinery, no five centuries in which to transmit and redact, in which to develop a new *poesis* for prayer or a new imaginative methodology for midrash. Given this predicament we can ill afford to rush to prayer and midrash without first formulating the questions appropriately designated as theological. Before we can repledge our troth to the ancient God or present him with our complaint—these twin stances of our modern prayer and protest—we must make certain that it is still the ancient God whom we seek.

Theology is the discipline that enables an unleisured time to compress its questions within the historical maelstrom. Those ancient times, before scripture was settled and the midrashim multiplied, were—if not preliterate—surely mythic. The traditions were oral before they became written and the oral transmission was mythic in character. Theology is a discipline of holographing the myth, obliging the myth to assert its contradictory claim and obliging us to winnow it that it may endure through us until the age of our poets dawns. Insisting upon inditing the holocaust as poetry in the absence not of poets (for we have many poets of the holocaust), but of poets possessed and made mad, has al-

ready produced enough mediocre liturgy and has not yet
found a way of adapting our great holocaust—someone like
Paul Celan—for the speaking of new liturgy. Liturgical
poetry is, after all, different from even the greatest of secular
poetry, not necessarily greater but assuredly different. The
way of making poetry out of the martyrologies of Israel is an
art of condensation and stripping to the bare bones of the
matter. But it could be done then—in the past of the
people—because the assumptions of the people about the
nature of its God and its experience of him was clear and
unmuddled. It is not so now. Any formulation which makes
the terms of God's relation to the holocaust comparable to
the formulations which were used by the medieval
payyetanim would be for us a scandal. We can bear the mysterious beauty of the *Unetaneh tokef kedushat ha-Yom* because we remove ourselves from the event through which
Rabbi Amnon of Mayence passed. We are not slain as they
were slain and we can speak of martyrdom and holiness
objectified through their pain. But dare we involve God in
the event of the *tremendum* in the same way as we involve
him in the mighty events of the Crusade massacres. We
know enough to say in our hearts that neither are we like
them nor is our faith the same as theirs. And if not, then
different is our God. And if not different, then no God of ours.
And if different, which God and who is our God?

Beyond all these considerations then, we must return
again and again to break our head upon the *tremendum* of
the abyss, a phenomenon without analogue, discontinuous
from all that has been, new beginning for the human race
that knew not of what it was capable, willing to destroy and
to be destroyed. We must create a new language in which to
speak of this in order to destroy the old language which, in
its decrepitude and decline, made facile and easy the demonic descent. When the preparations are completed, then
the new beginning of the race which started in that quintes-

sential perfection of the abyss must be thought (lest it be considered unthinkable) and redescribed (lest it be considered indescribable) and reconnected to the whole of the past (lest the abyss never be closed) and projected into the future (lest the future imagine it has no share in that past). In that way, first by separating the *tremendum* from all things and descending into the abyss, then by rejoining the *tremendum* to the whole experience of mankind as end-point of the abyss and new beginning of the race, it is possible to link again the death camps, the *tremendum* of the abyss, to the *mysterium tremendum* of God who is sometimes in love with creation and its creatures and sometimes, it must initially be thought, indifferent to their fate.

· 2 ·

THE TREMENDUM AS CAESURA
A Phenomenological Comment on the Holocaust

It is of the nature of the human that we live on two sides always: one illuminated, the other remaining in darkness; one side ardent in the pursuit of clarity and understanding (encouraged as both are by illumination), the other side muddled and confused; the one a pioneer of hope, while on the other despair couples with defeat. These bivalences of the human exist and they can be multiplied, each tentative of optimism muted by a contention of fatality. Moreover, these contrarieties inhere in the human, for there is little question that man is the riven species, given to dreams and hopes precisely in the degree of his dissatisfactions and imperfection.

The human prospect is grand and miserable and it is that familiar condition that religion addresses (believing itself enabled, by a different preachment, to shave—even if not to remove—the horns of the human dilemma) or that theology undertakes to reconcile by compelling one to the domination of the other. The grandeur and misery of the human nonetheless endure. It was obviously the power of ancient dualisms that they elaborated as contradiction without unity what was perceived by ordinary human beings to be

irreconcilable polarities of their situation: bifurcated creature in a bifurcated universe, man doubled in a universe that
is doubled, fractured man, prisoner of contradiction in a
universe no less cut in two.

Release from the bondage of contradiction is a form of
salvation, for such redemption clarifies absolutely (unlike
ordinary information which only clarifies relativities). Some
redemptions bind up our wounds; others, however, open
them and these so completely that from that time thereafter
the work of binding up and restoration becomes more difficult to effect and more difficult to accept.

The wounds of our present world (ours because we live in
it and are obliged recipients of its history) are nonetheless
wounds of the here below and real no less completely for
being of the here below and no less cruel and definitive
wounds for being of our making in what is affirmed by faith
to be a world of God's creation.

I

The *tremendum* of this century is a specific *tremendum*. As
such, it expresses an historical delimitation despite the fact
that the resonance of the term suggests an eruption of such
immensity that it is conceptually unlimited. We recognize,
however, in the very using of the term that no *tremendum* is
actually unlimited. It begins and it comes to an end. Like an
earthquake or a volcano, its tremor precedes its destructiveness and its after-shock recollects the destructiveness which
has passed. It is, so to speak, naturally bracketed off and
separated from the growth and decline of ordinary events in
our world. Where the *tremendum* is reducible to its historical
lineaments it loses its force as unlimited immensity. It becomes a metaphor. Any historical event regarded as beyond
comprehension, even if comprehension will one day be
achieved, is able to be called *tremendum*, but such usage is
improper and its employment in such an epistemological

context wastes the power of its immensity as event and its immensity as category.

Tremendum is used by me for the mysterious only, in precisely the sense which Rudolf Otto originally intended it. In my usage, however, the mysterious *tremendum* is not Otto's *mysterium tremendum*, the immense mystery. The phrase is reversed, my emphasis falling not upon the mystery as such but its immensity. It is the immensity of the event that is mysterious but its nature is not mystery.

I am not unaware of the neo-logistic employment to which I have put the otherwise generally unfamiliar Latin adjective, *tremendum*. Why *tremendum* at all? Would not immensity suffice, or extremity, or vastness, all forms of the same reality which may stand the reader to the same kind of recognition. Possibly, but not quite. *Tremendum*, as the other estranging adjectives that Otto employed, enjoyed the power and authority of a telluric urgency, an ancient language supplying Western man once again with fresh words by which to articulate our sense of the unfathomable otherness of God; and with that discernment of divine awesomeness and awfulness, a corresponding recognition of human debility, worthlessness, incapacity, and weakness before its mysterious power and authority. Otto's use of these categories of description, drawn as they principally are from the formulations of Hebrew scripture, suggest an intimacy of connection between the divine and the human which, however alienating and estranging it may on occasion become, carries with it an affective, caring relation no less profound. Otto sees the issue as one of driving off that a person may be drawn near, a dialectic in which intimacy covers both gestures—the numinal terror of human distance from God and the fear and trembling in which God is approached and addressed, lover to beloved.

The *tremendum* to which I address myself is, unlike the *tremendum* of divine mystery, no messenger from beyond our world. If Otto spoke of the *mysterium tremendum* as having something *grausam* about it, he referred to the grisly dimension of the numinal, its unearthly quality, its aspect of fright, estrangement, uncommonness, terror which follows from the divine insertion into our world. The *tremendum* of this century, quite unlike the immensity of the divine, although no less imperious, awesome, or commanding is mysterious because it exceeds the discernible causalities of history to which its apparent configuration refers. It gathers up the premises of history, but exceeds them. In some sense, therefore, such *tremenda* as these transcend their origins and determinants.* The dimension of exceeding determinable causalities alludes as well to an appropriate commentary upon Otto's almost optimistic espousal of the numinal in religion, for my usage of *tremendum* is intended to suggest that a portion of the fascination and dread which both holds us before God and affrights us in the divine presence may share something with the demonic *tremendum*. However much we may be fascinated and in awe of divine power, we are not less fascinated and in awe of monstrous power, that is, the power and works of the monstrous.

In all the senses intended by me—as neologism in its application to the death camps, in its aspect as commentary and gloss upon its earlier employment as an adjectival component of the divine mystery, and lastly as a reality of subscension and hence frightening and awesome in itself—the *tremendum* of an historical event is a reality that makes claim upon us. It is not a dependent reality whose power derives from something else. If the *tremendum* could be reduced to its causes or folded back into its antecedents, it would have a conditional reality which would diminish its

---

* Transcend is used here only in the sense of "to exceed": in fact, it may be the case as I proposed in chapter 1 (p. 22) that the appropriate neologism for the poetic direction of this *tremendum* is that it "subscends" its origins, digging deeper into the infernal abyss of human and historical negativity.

stature as *tremendum*. It would be less than *tremendum*, however much it might appear to us to be, for the moment, *tremendum*. I would not use *tremendum* to elicit the ontological station of other monsters of this century, however monstrous or horrible we might agree them to be, because the universally acknowledged is for precisely that fact of universality and acceptance not *tremendum*. The authentic *tremendum* resists; its ontological thrust is blunted, repudiated, even denied. It is a horror that exceeds the category of horror and is, for that reason, inadmissible to some, even to many, whereas the horror acknowledged by all (the dropping of atom bombs or the use of genetically deforming contaminants in Vietnam) is in part neutralized and divested of its horror. Another way of putting this contention is this: it is accepted by everyone informed that atomic warfare can destroy the world; the widespread acknowledgment of the undeniable possibility of complete destruction introduces the *tremendum* as real possibility into the field of reason, since complete destruction is a comprehensible idea. Since such destruction, if it occurs, will happen to *all* it is as though it will happen to *no one in particular*. Its universality and its general acceptance deprive it of the vivacity of the particular and the irrationality of the procedures of selection.

Atomic destruction is no *tremendum* for us although it may well be the case that before God—and only before God—it is the single *tremendum* that may be recognized as such, since it is the final defeat of creation. But in our perspective (human, not Jewish), what has finality for God has no relevance for us. In our perspective, the mysterious *tremendum* of this century is the one that has no universal acceptance nor widespread recognition; to the contrary, it is one against whose claim many rebel, not only those who share the persuasion of the victimizers but also those who share the condition of its victims. It is a *tremendum* of such particularity and specificity that many may argue its interpretation or deny its existence. It is consequently a *tremendum* that elicits panic, terror, fear, awe, and ongoing fascination.

II

History until this century could be described as the product of lapsed memory, repeating itself endlessly because always perceived in partiality, secured by the rationalization of justifying and excusing ideology which could not (for being ideology) be set down as objective truth, even accurate statistics. The past has been no less the theater of barbarism than our own age, but for the fact that it was unable to secure and transmit the condensation of memory as brute fact. Before, there could be ambiguity and obscurantism; teaching that rationalized the murderer and made guilty the murdered, vast hordes of nomadic anonymity overriding settled nations in their turn to settle down and be overridden. The nineteenth century reconstrued the ancient teaching and articulated cyclicity and eternal return; although the wheels of historical fortune were not heard, they turned inexorably, prepared relentlessly.

It is different now. The immense system and intentionality of the murderer is clear. There is no ideology, no rationalization, no absence of document which will allow the debris of history to abrade memory and efface it. The murderers and their descendants know; the murdered and their descendants have been informed. The wound of the survivor is as permanent as is his redemption by clarification. Illusion is stripped away and with it the commonplace perplexity with which theologies before these decades have bothered themselves, that of evil.

Evil exists. It is no longer understood as the absence of good, privation, a lapsarian abnegation, a void of conscience, a characterological defect. Any and all of these modalities of glossing the content of the *tremendum* have disappeared.

The difficulty of interpreting the ethical content of historical cataclysm has been the reluctance to regard evil as substantive, as ontologically affirmative, as real presence. There was a double difficulty implicit in notions of theodicy: the inability to affirm evil as having substance in a creation made good by absolute goodness, but as well and tributary to it, manifest evil had to be denied substantive reality, since substance itself was considered the ground of the real and an evidentiary certification of goodness. It followed that evil was described by the language of negation and denial, emptiness and void, the terms of insubstantiality merging with the characteristics of negativity and the metaphoric coloration of night, darkness, emptiness underscoring a metaphysical diminution and absence. But these colligations of language are neither indispensable nor necessary. Evil can be substantial presence, real, making claim (and hence affirming), exerting power (and hence an order of being). Evil may be accorded ontological station without our risking, as traditionally feared, that the universe would be delivered to its sovereignty and divine goodness denied. It is part of our inherited view of the *Satan*, the adversary, that our language of evil is partially mythological, obliging centuries which constructed the universe according to an epistemology of essence and accident to consider *real* evil as though it possessed a power equal to that of God. However, all that is contended at this point is that evil is a real force, that its negativity and destructiveness are no less an aspect of the human structure than is that structure's potency for good, that the human labor to identify and subdue manifestations of evil remains as decisive as the human energy to augment and create. Evil has ontic reality no less than the good.

If it may be imagined that human beings are little lower than the angels or, as Lessing thought, "limited gods," as respects our capacity for virtue, man may be little higher than devils as respects our capacity for evil. Otherwise stated, however much it may have been thought necessary to protect God by denying the reality of evil, it is now incumbent that we protect man by the assertion of evil's authenticity and power. Too much inadequate thinking may have been wasted on preserving an archaic theodicy (and by implication an archaic theism) without attending to the increasingly precise evidence which modern civilization offers that both God and man are in need of rethinking and redescription.

The difficulty of religious profession is that for many (both those who profess as well as those who refuse profession) the sovereignty of evil has become more real and immediate and familiar than God. The question for these is not how can God abide evil in the world, but how can God be affirmed meaningfully in a world where evil enjoys such dominion. The task of rethinking, therefore, is not to make cogent a rationalization of evil (a rationalization that would ultimately render its presence chimeric) but rather, accepting its reality, to estimate what consequence it has for our thinking about the nature, existence, and action of God.

The procedure of reformulation entails a reversal in my own thinking which I suspect has been long overdue. The way for thought about God and God's world must be made vastly more difficult and treacherous than I imagined a generation ago when I was preparing *The Natural and the Supernatural Jew*. Then, I imagined that it was a defect of vocation that inhibited the Jew's self-recognition as the messianic bearer; I did not take notice—although the debris was all about me—that the fragile, even insubstantial, character of Jewish religious thinking in the contemporary world derived in part from the fact that it had no language with which to speak of evil (other than by exhibition and denunciation) and hence hardly took account of its distortion. It continued to speak—as I spoke—of theological covenants with the creative, as though theology could continue to use a language developed in a world which did not recognize, much less identify, the evil accumulating in all things. Some of my more trenchant critics (in those days Richard Rubinstein was among the most scandalous but quite possibly the most accurate) noted that I had constructed a modern theology without dealing with evil, either in itself or in its horrific manifestation as *tremendum. The Natural and the Supernatural Jew* retains its merit as a clear and closely argued attack on Jewish theological innocence, but it is nonetheless an easy book (easy, not facile), making the way cleaner and less encumbered by inadequate and poorly formulated doctrine, but still defective in its perception of evil and consequently in its reading of the historical. Then, I tried to take the Jews out of history (thereby solving the problem of history, by leaving it a problem for Christians) and, by regarding evil as a modality of the historical, I secured the Jewish people from ever being thought to have done evil, insuring that for the future they could be its victims, never its perpetrators. But clearly, such a view of history and evil—whatever its rhetorical advantages—leaves something to be desired. If one is a people within history (as natural Jews), one's vocation as supernatural may serve it as criterion and source of judgment, but cannot protect the historical Jew from suffering and doing according to the distortions of finite perspective, limited access to truth, and that haste and impatience with the ultimate that leaves all human action under the dominion of partiality and hence of evil. In those days I cordoned the Jew from evil without having understood what it was that had occurred in the *tremendum.* I was shattered by the recognition of evil and hence unable to take account of it. I think of Gyges' ring of truth, but I understand that if the light glows upon its surface, one may still be blinded and rendered foolish and self-deceiving.

Richard Rubinstein was right. I had ignored Auschwitz, imagining that somehow I had escaped. But he was not right in that imputation. I did not imagine that I had escaped (or that any Jew of the non-European diaspora had escaped). But I was struck dumb and I turned aside (this is documented more efficiently in my fiction *In the Days of Simon Stern*, than it can be argued here)—and that amounts to the same thing: avoidance. The *tremendum* cannot be avoided; nor does it matter whether the non-Jew shares in the welter of the *tremendum* of the Jews, if only non-Jews regard *tremendum* as a configuration whose name is called in our language one event and in theirs another. Auschwitz or Hiroshima or Vietnam or Cambodia or Uganda—what does it matter as long as each person knows the *tremendum* that bears his name; and it is one name only, for the rest what endures beyond the name and binds each human being in abjectness and torment to the other is that the configurations overlay, the *tremendum* of the Jews becomes the *tremendum* of the nations. Over the abyss which each hollows out of history, human beings renew their sense of themselves as creatures beleaguered by their destinies as Jews or Christians or Africans or Buddhists or whatever name is called victim and murderer. I refuse, in other words, to allow the compromise of uniqueness by the procedures of analogy. When Jews insist that the *tremendum* of the death camps is unique they speak correctly, but no less the other butchered peoples of the earth, butchered no less in their being and hence no less irrationally and absolutely. Every genocidal *tremendum* is unique to the victims; it is only those who feel upon themselves the breath of guilt and contamination that the insistence falls to argue with the claims of uniqueness. The Cambodian does not tell the Jew that Auschwitz is not unique—it is the calm West that makes such announcements, denying caesura to the one as to the other by making of their virtual self-condemnation an equivalency which allows guilt to seep through and evaporate. I cannot allow the one or the other: I cannot make the *tremendum* of the Jews so distinctive that nothing can be said of it—language requires, for the barest use, some measure of similitude, some *analogia;* however, I do not imagine that similitude and analogy are the same as identity. They allow us to talk of such catastrophe; they allow us to speak of the abyss but not to fill it.

Beyond the easy book of 1962, I have tried several times to describe the purview and method of Jewish thinking in the aftermath of the *tremendum. The Myth of the Judeo-Christian Tradition* (1970) was a self-stripping, an argument of divestment, putting distance between myself and Christianity, by allowing myself the opportunity—giving myself indirect permission, so to speak—to despise Christianity and Christendom in the open. I made clear then (and I repeat now) that never persons, but ideologies bore the weight of my enmity as I believe not Jews, but Judaism should receive the intent of Christian enmity. Enmity does not mean enemies, if persons have the courage to risk articulating their sense of destiny and the possibility of history as ongoing; as long as they dream to themselves, dreams turn to ash and fury, but when they speak openly their dreams of faith, it is possible to know the ground on which human beings stand. It is then that enmity becomes its opposite, as fundamental a source of hope as love. Beyond *The Myth*, I worked between a poorly constructed fiction *The Carpenter Years*, which set forth some of the premises of Jewish anti-Christianity (what I have elsewhere referred to as "envy of the Gentiles"), and *In the Days of Simon Stern*, an obsessive, maddened novel of Jewish rage, Jewish enmity, and Jewish hope. But of the *tremendum* as such I spoke not at all. For nearly a generation I could not speak of Auschwitz, for I had no language that tolerated the immensity of the wound: I worked around the abyss and I made of it imaginings and nightmares, but only once, in the lecture "Thinking the Tremendum," * did I approach the matter. Even then I found myself driven to recoil, not because the vision was untrue, but rather because the vision remained vision. That lecture succeeded in limning the parameters of the abyss but found them beyond compass and containment. It was a probing that left me dry with rage and without hope. Whatever its merits, the argument remained locked within the terms of historical inquiry, a marking out of terrain, replete with markers and the surveyor's annotation of sightings, but without an overall scheme that encouraged the colonization of its barren landscape.

The analysis that I propose now engages the issues raised by the earlier topographic abstract: the questions are no longer those of historical and literary identification but rather the reality of evil and the existence of God, the extremity of evil and the freedom of man, the presentness of evil and the power of God. My thinking is, as will be evident, dialectical, although the dialectic is neither a sufficient nor a persuasive method of proceeding. However, dialectical inquiry is appropriate to the spoken word where all depends upon the audible yes and no, leaving the power of the copulative conjunction, the indispensable link, to emerge from the ontological annotation that succeeds dialectic. The whole to which my argument will press is a unity which sustains the rhythm of each affirmation and negation, in which I hope, negativity will emerge as no longer necessarily evil and evil will be perceived to be not simply negative, but no less an argument in which the God who emerges as possible to thought beyond the *tremendum* is no longer the God of traditional theology, while remaining nonetheless the divinity of whom Thales of Miletus observed, "God is the oldest of beings."

---

* "Thinking the Tremendum" appears in this volume, extensively revised, as the introductory chapter to this book.

III

To suggest that the future of Jewish theology in the time beyond the *tremendum* be explored is to assume that there is a possible connection between thought and the *tremendum;* moreover, it is to conjure the possibility that if the *tremendum* has more than a tangential or accidental impact upon Jewish thought (and hence, ultimately, upon the content of Jewish belief), then it is something that can be compassed and interpreted by thought. Is thought then commensurate or incommensurate to the *tremendum?* That is to say, can an intellectual aptitude encompass the *tremendum* as an historical event or is the *tremendum as historical event* of such complexity that, at best, the tools of historical retrieval can succeed only in the development of intermediate judgments of social, political, psychological origin. Thought may describe the limit-implications of the *tremendum,* but its ability to pierce the borders of historical determination and caprice to assertions about general significance and meaning may be regarded by some as hopeless, given the unavoidable narrowness of the single thinker's viewpoint or the denigration of thought itself as too cool or too dispassionate a procedure for estimating such historical immensity. Obviously, for those who disrespect thinking or find its methods and attenuations too slow and plodding when the earth cries out for justice I have no contention. They are right to set thought aside, although they run the risk that by ignoring its deliberations, real evil will neither have the confinement of understanding nor the prospect which I hold—that it have its portion before a real God. Again, I understand their point of view. No God is worth a single child's life. How much more so untold children? I would agree with this caveat as well, if I also agreed that life can be winnowed with such equivalences, with such an overwhelming dramaturgy, for history nowhere presents such symmetrical historical options as God or your babe.

The antagonism to deliberative scrutiny of the *tremendum* has a variety of origins, not the least relevant of which is Kai Erikson's observation about the psychological condition of its survivors, who, having outlived its destructiveness, are prone forever after to overestimate "the perils of their situation, if only to compensate for the fact that they underestimated those perils once before." The mentality of the survivor—and Judaism is a tradition which has apostrophized the miracle of survival from its very beginnings, underscoring in each generation the sign of the Exodus and its symbolic adumbration in each historical searing—consists in a continuous self-rebuke, wherein the past is repeatedly examined for danger signs overlooked and the future is read without the normal ability, in Erikson's phrase, to "screen out the signs of danger" from the line of sight. But more than such psychological resistance is the pervasive popular conviction that theology, with its unavoidable eccentricity of language and its insistence upon pinning down the reality in focus, makes the *tremendum* into an object—a mere object—when it is regarded by survivors and memorialists alike to be so charged a reality as to require that the extremities of subjectivity and passion be engaged in its evocation.

It is out of regard, therefore, for these sensibilities that I have adopted the term *tremendum*. The term is allusive; it encourages the awareness of alien immensity, acknowledging the anguish of the survivors and their ongoing apprehensiveness, while refusing to foreclose the possibility that it is, at one and the same time, a destructive event that uniquely occurred (and therefore a proper object of study), as well as a reality that endures and continues to make assaultive claim upon subjective, impassioned, even unconscious awareness.

If we stand on the contention that thought is essentially incapable of compassing the *tremendum*, that it must fall silent and dumb before its monstrousness, there are additional consequences which extend far beyond the matter of personal decision, emotional tolerance, and consciousness. The first and most pressing is that the past that pressed against us before the *tremendum* is annihilated; by implication, those who would make thought ineffectual or the event unthinkable succeed not only in obliterating the past as the legacy of continuity and instruction but also destroy the past-oriented purview of historical consciousness itself. If the *tremendum* is an event unparalleled, unique in every characteristic dimension of uniqueness and if, as is signaled by our language, *tremendum* means historical immensity for which there is neither a satisfactory analogue nor historical model, the history of the past becomes irrelevant.

The judgment that thought is inadequate to the *tremendum* is, in one sense, based upon a logical fallacy, for it is never suggested that thought can number six million particularities or, for that matter, the hundred million slain in this century's wars of skill and ideology. The fact that the mind cannot contain such particularity is not a mark of the incommensurability of thought, but only of memory's inability to particularize each loss. The containment of the numbers is not the issue nor even the diabolic planning and imagination which devised these holocausts, but rather (as Erich Kahler observed in his premonitory *Man the Measure*) the triumph of technics by which procedures of dehumanization and distanciation were brought to their perfection. The evil is remarked less in its passion than in its coldness. Indeed, if the *tremendum* cannot be thought, more than the past would have been lost and loss of the past would be loss enough.

If the holocaust is allowed to stand as a *mysterium*, indeed, a mysterious *tremendum* unavailable to thought, unsusceptible of any intellectual seizure and identification, the profound risk is run that an historical event is made absolute and therefore necessary, overturning all other historical events whose occurrence is contingent and whose meaning is tributary. Or the holocaust is allowed to stand as a *mysterium*, indeed, a *mysterium tremendum* precisely because it is not historical and derives its force and arbitrariness from the metaphysical structure of the universe, no less absolute and necessary, overturning thereby all other metaphysical structures including God whose existence is claimed by classic theism to be alone absolute and necessary. In summary, if the holocaustal *tremendum* is necessary, it is necessary evil in contradiction and negation of God (who traditionally is alone thought to be necessary) or coeval and coexistent with God, since it enjoys a metaphysical identity accorded no other reality besides God. If the project of absolutizing the holocaust is pushed much further than it has been already, it is made twin of the divine, indeed, a function of the divine (or the divine a function of evil's naturalness) and a partner of its relation to the world. Such a radical extension of the argument from holocaustal ontologies ends by making the *tremendum* no different than divine and divine truth.

The extremities of the argument are implicated, on the one hand, by those who have expressed the hope that the holocaust had no meaning, that is to say, conveyed no historical judgment, that it was an emptiness, a void ("meaning" to be understood in such usage as significant, interpretive truth, bearing insight from past to future). In such a view the holocaust is neither philosophically nor theologically relevant, except as exemplifying the void before which we gape in disbelief. But on the other side, there are those who suggest that the holocaust—far from being without meaning—contains absolute meaning. Indeed, the holocaust is regarded as a decisive event by which the whole of the past and the future is henceforth to be marked out and scanned.

Implicit in either the denial of meaning or the absolutization of meaning is a reflection upon the historical reality to which the holocaust adhered. The holocaust in fact may have been of history, but its reading and significance may be trans-historical and its metaphysical truth may be transcendent of history. We begin however by retracing the evisceration of the transcendent from history.

Historical existence has been stripped of sacral implication for more than two centuries. This is not to hold a brief for the modalities of its improper sanctification, for my interest is not in the investment of the historical with sacerdotal sanctities but rather with the uncompromised openness of the historical to both the sacred and the ordinary. The profane has passed its judgment; whether Church or Synagogue manipulate the saeculum, not the Holy but the profane triumphs, not the believing people but their authoritative powers are victorious. The Church year, for example, which Rosenstock-Huessy elaborated or calendrical holiness which Franz Rosenzweig described had not only a visionary prospect but a didactic annotation of the historical past at issue. The human in the human being counts for little. Submitted to anonymous, manipulative, depersonalized control, the individual and his free imagination are flayed raw. Within a stripped and naked saeculum the holocaust can be only relatively situated. An historical order without prevenient limits set by the Holy is, at most, relatively disastrous; absolute disaster to be meaningful occurs only within a perspective that continues to acknowledge the absolute. Otherwise employed, lacking the texture of being, absolute "anything" is always rhetorical language, since the affirmed absolute is absolute only in relation to the lesser, remaining relative in relation to the superior and true absolute whose presence and power have been lost from view. In short, then, given a historical vision or social doctrine which allows of no transcendence, no openness before absolute claim, no nexus between the human and the divine, what has occurred as *tremendum* is, at best, a malign fortuity which, as its sufferers, we force upon the world's attention as though it were of significance to everyone or, abashed, we deny it meaning, hoping from the benign indifference of secular toleration that the accident will not become normative. The dialectic of the dilemma suggests that whichever side is espoused we are endangered: if we describe the *tremendum* as the inevitable product of a stripped saeculum, unconstrained by the limits conscience sets to the demonic imagination, the holocaust is rendered an absolute relative, that is, an event marked by perfect relativity, relativity of value, meaning, truth, precisely as its conception and machinery effect the total humiliation of man. It is absolute because it serves as the model—comprehensive, logical, obsessively organized and consummated. On the other hand, if it is hastily transformed into a theological repudiation of God, a defiance flung before divinity, an historical rebellion against his silent intimacy, it emerges as a relative absolute, since it makes the contention that God is incomplete, inadequate, impotent before the domain of history and, therefore, given its assertion of providential solicitude and concern, no longer God.

What is common to both viewpoints is the immense seriousness with which history is regarded. History is treated as though it were self-interpreting, as though the adduction of history carries with it the force of clarification and proof. Constantly counseled to consult the historical to chasten optimism or reprove despair, history becomes for us the advisor of the secular imagination, indeed, the new divinity of events to be set beside biological, physical, cosmological contentions. Clearly, however, the inability of historical description and analysis to compass the holocaust is one of the central reasons for the assertion of its incommensurability to thought. The holocaust cannot be thought because it cannot be exhausted by historical narration. It remains elusive, uncontained, a putative mystery because the categories by which such immensities are grasped seem inadequate and trivial.

Before this century, intellectual projects seemed well scaled and hence possible. Even where God was set forth as a problem of mind, the God in view was easily reduced to the scale of mind. *Our* history, however, is one apparently without a canon, without reliable *docta* of exegesis, without even an ideology of national *hubris* supplying its rationale and interpretation. We have neither a contemporary Hegel nor a Marx; however much we make appeal to them, our discourse of longing or rage consists in knocking upon their closed doors beseeching that our categories be admitted. Instead, our times turn to revisionist instruction about history, accumulating the information dropped from previous renditions, obscured as they were by clouds of ideology and interests. Revisionist history (written with no less passion than those of national self-interpretation and excuse) has the purpose of filling the foreground with visible events so large (and yet without previous advocacy) that they could be ignored in the nineteenth century's rush to national exaltation.

Our predicament at the borders of the *tremendum* and in its aftermath is that the familiar disciplines of interpretation seem compromised or ineffective: philosophic thought appears debarred, the social consensus seems dehumanized, historical identification and description seems lacking in theoretical grandeur and comprehensiveness.

IV

It has been necessary to begin with the watershed of the *tremendum*. The *tremendum* clearly marks and will continue to mark the cleavage between the conventional liberal expectations of nineteenth-century Judaism and the future of

Judaism. The reason that the holocaustal *tremendum* has, and will continue to have for generations to come, a decisive place in Jewish experience and thought is that it ended, once and for all, the terrestrial expectations of social assimilation and cultural accommodation, all dreams of the project of enlightenment and emancipation and the surge of moralist progressivism which dominated the liberal strain of European Judaism. Beyond the holocaust, the only liberalism possible is one stripped of all religious and theological content. Optimism (which is not hope), progressivism (which is not realistic), and liberalism (which is not realism) are attitudinal doctrines which conceal an ideology that has made frequent pretense to being a metaphysic (i.e., to being part of the nature of things rather than a wholly contingent intellectual outcropping), while remaining an ideology invested with piety. Liberalism (and in its radicalization, Marxism) may well be the fallen messianism of the Jews, the familiar secular inversion of Jewish utopian hope, but liberalism is predicated upon assumptions regarding the nature of man and his educable potentiality which the *tremendum* destroyed. Before the *tremendum*, Jews could not have imagined that a people could produce high cultural achievement and surrender to a politics of monstrosity; Jews could not believe that, having effected the rites of passage from ethnic enclave to cultural universalism, their lineage would still be traced by blood to their discovery and murder. The liberalism of the Jews—that analogical rendering of the message of the prophets—undid their judgment of the real, for having mellowed their theology into social optimism, Jews tended to misread the gestures of emancipation as good will and the recrudescence of anti-Semitism as the work of malign and unregenerate ideologists. The fundamental error of Jewish liberalism and its collateral reinforcement by Jewish traditionalists (who often allowed themselves to be coopted by the political right in return for favors of social noncompliance, which amounted to little more than the willingness of the Establishment to render eccentric and therefore· malleable the nonparticipatory wishes of the Orthodox) lies in the benign misreading of the emancipatory signs and gestures of Christian Europe in the century before the *tremendum,* and a consequent indifference to the crying need for a *Jewish* theology of politics and secular duty.

In the holocaust is a configuration of evil; it writes large what should have been recognized all along—that the oppository, destructive character of evil drains of credibility every notion of an ongoing teleology of the good that was required by the rational optimisms and social Darwinisms of the nineteenth century. No longer can it be asserted that the world grows better or that mankind improves. It can be said that techniques mature, capacities sophisticate, gifts of manipulation become refined, but these are all optimisms of potency, not of acts. The technics improve, but their manipulators remain unchanged. A liberalism founded upon a notion of an inner will to self-redemption and moral improvement is finished for the time being—as long that is as Jews and Christians and other civilized human beings remember the history of evil. History is mindless, but its incident nonetheless reminds. Unfortunately the history of our times is "unpleasant" and not at all memorable. It is always more palatable to construe its record (even though in our century such will be an ingenious feat) as the course of virtue and tranquillity, rather than as the legend of violence and destruction. It is, it seems, a natural law of memory that virtue is retained as lively impression, while the workings of evil are repressed to the dark shadows of the unconscious where only conflict and torment hold sway. It is perhaps for this reason that the capacity to read dreams and nightmares has always been an arcane and mysterious genius, since it is not from our dreams and nightmares that our optimistic

fantasies of the world derive, but rather from our daylight
wishes that we misconstrue history and its course.

V

The traditional formulations of theodicy, those that we have
inherited as the unavoidable sentiment that textures community and belief, come down particularly hard on the reality of evil. Evil emerges (unlike the good) as defective intel-
lection and judgment, a failure of perception and clarification. What reality evil enjoys is diminished before the promise of its future conquest—the dragon is always slain, the
evil kingdom vanquished, the deadly minions overwhelmed.
Evil, like the dead branch, is always fated to be cut down.
But such liturgic metaphor, whatever hope it sparks, en-
forces the expectation of cumulative triumph, as though evil
upon evil will be vanquished until the auguries of the mil-
lennium gather.

The reading of this century is different. The evil of this
age, as it was during the expulsion of Spanish Jewry in 1492,
is crystallized as a symbolic cloture which, however past, is
not done. The holocaust is fixed to a time but resonates endlessly and without end. It is seen as ultimate evil, intending
by such ultimacy a consummate destructiveness. The
holocaust, in its immediacy, constellates everything that we
mean by evil and, as such, is a perfected figuration of the
demonic. In this respect, it is borne into the life of memory,
not as a discrete and finite episode that comes into being and
passes away, accident among accidents, but as an order of
being which sinks roots deep into the human *passio* and,
though cut off, lurks in the spirit available to succor and
renascence. It is not, as were the earlier catastrophes of
Jewish history, the concomitant of national disaster or the
aggravated *hubris* of a triumphalist Church, but the expression of ordinary secular corruption raised to immense pow-

ers of magnification and extremity. The *tremendum* defied expectation, defied predictability, defied hope—not the murderous enmity of Babylon or Imperial Rome, not the paranoid vulnerability of Christian princes, not the peasant populism of the Cossack *hetman*. From all of these, exterior authorities to whom Jewry had no loyalty or obligation, it was no surprise that terror would arise—hence the incredible willingness with which Jewry assimilated the disaster of its depredations as merited by sins and waywardness. But that the *tremendum* should derive its power and authentication from the secular state, from societies of high culture and reputed civilization, from the descendants of the era of its own emancipation, in whom Jewry had reposed trust and faith, is and remains astonishing.

The *tremendum* is ultimate; its symbolic resonance permanent; its repetition is the continuous assurance of its potency; its very ultimacy is prefiguration. But it is not, for all its being ultimate, final. It is ultimate because it comprehends and articulates all negativity and contradiction, but it is still not final. Finality and ultimacy differ crucially. Ultimacy entails the formal and configurational character of the real event, whereas finality describes its intention and its goal. It is one thing to speak of the *tremendum* as ultimate, quite another to affirm its finality. If final, *everything* is intended to evil and we must conclude that our affairs are run, if not by blind caprice, then most surely by a malign divinity.

Among the implications of ultimacy—in this case, our experience of ultimate evil—is that, as its bearers (whether as actual survivors or as active memorialists or as those implicated, present or absent, sufferers or rememberers, in its demonic purview), we are obliged (as we would be by any decisive experience) to reappraise our situation in its aftermath. Some of the procedures of estimation and excogitation remain the same as those employed for less charged events, since we continue, as human beings, to feel, perceive, think, and reflect upon the *tremendum* as an *objectivum*, applying to it criteria of evidence and analysis (cool and measured) at seeming variance with its charged and relentless presence. We compel ourselves to distance, to consider probatively, to amass evidence, to take testimony and record the recollection of witnesses and survivors. In other words, despite the fact that the mere impression—the photographs of stacked corpses or hollow-eyed starvelings—is enough to blast reason and precipitate rushed judgment, we oblige ourselves to step back, to bend backwards not for the sake of doing justice to the murderers but of showing mercy to all those of us—Jews and Gentiles—who must continue to live in a world where such has taken place and is henceforth possible again. We deal with the *tremendum* as ultimate always, but we do not yield to its finality. Of course, in a world stripped of divinity, it is not only ultimate, but final, despair transforming pessimism into a normative decree. To the extent, however, that we maintain our connection as Jews with our own history, we are compelled by it to recognize the respects in which the *tremendum* of this century resembles but is different from the catastrophes of old. We have no more choice than did the *rabbanim* after the destruction of the Temple and the beginning of the long exile or Jewish philosophers and kabbalists after the expulsion of Spanish Jewry: like our ancestors we are obliged to decide whether such catastrophes are compatible with our traditional notions of a beneficent and providential God. The past generations of Israel decided that they were. The question today is whether the same conclusion may be wrung from the data of the *tremendum*.

The dialectic of Jewish history is one that raises up to consciousness the obvious paradox of inherited Jewish doctrine, that a beneficent and caring God appears to have allowed his elected people to be brought to the borders of extinction. The solution of ancient days took a liturgic form ("For thy sake are we slain all the day") or quasi-theological form that interpreted national disaster as modalities of reproof and instruction. Such doctrine, an eloquent archaism at best, survived and continues to survive within Jewish fundamentalism but has no sensible reflection in reasonable theology. Beyond classical fundamentalism, the philosopher-kabbalists supplied a different orientation that sought to interpret the presence and potency of evil as the inevitable concomitant of creation, a portion of the creative process, evil being waste and waste the by-product of creation; the irrational detritus of creation moved by revelation to become historical remains still a portion of the divine beginning and unravelment of the divine self. Through such a kabbalistic reading, evil acquired, if not metaphysical reality as engaged potency, at least a portion in the procedures of creation, its negativity cadenced into the rhythm of creation.

Some portion of the historical past and the history of the intellectual procedures by which the past is ordered and retained endure for us as well. The *tremendum* is no order of pride that we would claim it for ourselves and for our times as its privilege. That it is part of our midst is acknowledgment of its energy and power, but that we are made more sadly unique by its occurrence is an untruth.

In summary to this juncture, it is argued that the *tremendum* is an evil portion of real history, that its reality as history is not sundered or torn free of its moorings in causality and aftermath, but that as an *objectivum* of Jewish theological consciousness it is to be perceived as bracketed and independent of its historical enmeshment, that it may be lifted out of temporality and regarded as an enduring pointer and symbol. It is then a reality with a double valence: an historical life which, however immense and monstrous, must be regarded as historical and a theological reality that insists upon a new reading of Jewish meaning. If it is only history, its life is as long as the life of memory and there is no command to memory that can be naturally enforced, even by good conscience; but if it is as well raised up as a monument out of time and installed as a metaphysical evidence that discloses something new about our relation to God and God's relation to creation, it acquires an ineffaceable eternity, an eternity no less an article of faith than the eternity of the Jewish people.

VI

I am no longer persuaded, as I once was, that Martin Buber was correct in his contention that there are no caesuras in Jewish history. Clearly, Buber's stand against historical caesura grew out of his polemical interpretation of Christianity. Buber regarded salvation out of incarnation and the empty tomb as an arbitrary insertion of the plumbline of eternity into the vortex of time, with the result that history was broken open to the pre-Christ and the post-Christ and the marking off within Judaism of prophetic figurations and posterior stubbornness. Buber's insistence therefore that Judaism has no midpoints, that Jewish history is cantilevered from its moorings in creation toward an unfixed endtime, was part of his intellecual momentum *contra Christiana* and, as such, is unexceptionable. And yet, although I feel impelled by the logic of my own argument to validate caesura, I do so with much hesitation and uncertainty.

Caesura was intended by Buber to describe a vertical insertion of the divine into history, a breaching of the historical by the eternal, a setting forth within history of a divine exposition as incarnational God-man. But caesura need not be only the descent of the dove; it can be a raising up and release of chthonic instinctualism as well, the terrestrial fission of caprice and the passivity of nature. Caesura in such a reversal can emerge from below, a verticality as infernal as incarnation may be divine. But what matters in caesura is not its content, but its rupture.

The content of the *tremendum* is always historical—its cruelties and murders; the caesura, however, is that the *tremendum* marks off and breaks. The caesura is the formal definer of holocaust, what makes it special, separable, ontic.

The *tremendum* is more than historical. It is an elaboration of the most terrible of Jewish fears—that the eternal people is not eternal, that the chosen people is rejected, that the Jewish people is mortal. If there is one incontestable article of the Jewish unconscious, it has been the mythos of indestructibility and the moral obligation of tenacity. Six years, nonetheless, nearly concluded three millennia of endurance. Is it a wonder that Jews should regard the *tremendum* as a caesural fissure that acquires with each decade a more and more profound meta-historical station as the counter-event of Jewish history, the source of its revisionist reconsideration and self-appraisal. No accounting, even in the most dreadful apocalyptic readings of modern history, adumbrated a structure of convergent causalities that might have yielded an event of such catastrophic destructiveness. The break is in our reading of the historical—that we are obliged to insert into the history of salvation, alongside ancient martyrologies (individual saints and heroes whose deaths provided two millennia with models of courage and steadfastness), a litany of faceless numbers that declare to us nothing but monstrousness.

And yet, however much it all seems clear, the wish to transform the *tremendum* into an event without analogue or historical echo, without forecastings or preludes, to make of it not only the paradigm of theological ultimacy but historical ultimacy may be called a rush to ontologize history. The holocaust is surely ours; against its background, we can verify no other event of comparable magnitude. The destruction of the Temple and the exile of Israel have already found their portion in the liturgic imagination, and there is no doubt that for classic Judaism it was a shattering and defining event that marked off a Judaism of the beforehand and the after, determining the end of a cult of silent acts and the beginning of a synagogue of prayer and study. For their consciousness it was caesura; but the insistence of the rabbis that the continuity be underscored, and the eternal life of Torah planted in their midst be tended without interruption, neutralized caesura and recast it as an instructive historical eruption. In our eyes, therefore, the destruction of the Temple in 70 C.E. was no caesura because the tradition took up the frayed ends of time and knotted them. It was no less with the catastrophic destruction of Sephardic Judaism, begun in 1391 and completed beyond the expulsion. Once again, a world came to an end and, once again, a mythos of incorporation and consolation emerged with which to supply a nexus and continuity, where previously only despairing caesura had been palpable. What is read as judgment, and received as the passion of the Jewish people, is transmuted, the agony of history lifted up into a reading that allowed to God vastly more complexity and interior movement than had been envisaged by the negative theologies that preceded it.

Historical extremity has compelled the tradition to rethink. Neither arguments over doctrine nor conflicts between theology and philosophy nor combat between religion and science moved Jewish thought to reformulate, but rather the aftermath of shattering historical events. Judaism has always been content to overhear the disputes of others and file the reconciliations they devise. What Judaism combats, the battlefield of its proper *agon*, is the historical.

VII

Until the *tremendum* it was possible to speak of Judaism among the world religions, of the Jewish people among the peoples of the world, of Jewish belief and practice in comparison with the beliefs and practices of other communities. It is still possible for others to continue as they have—to interpret their destinies against their past, to struggle for coherence and clarity under challenge from the erosive ideologies and competing doctrines of modernity, to devise stratagems of revision and reconstruction to account better for their vision of the world and its enhancement, because for them there is the prospect of time (no longer leisured time nor time rendered supple by the protection of powers and princes, but still time and the conviction of futurity). The Jew no longer has such time in his vision; he may have great time by the grace of God (a pious rhetoric) but it is not his to know (this, neither a piety nor rhetoric), for the Jew sees not time future in his length of days, but pierced and truncated time, time fissured by the *tremendum*. The Jew is the creature brought up short: if he wishes to continue in belief and expectation, if he wishes to transcend the historical situation toward clarity and knowledge, if he seeks to persevere in instruction and fidelity, he is obliged to take up the caesura and consider it the demarcating boundary to his life and thought.

If the *tremendum* is a caesura that marks off the Jew from his environment, nothing can be construed as though it had not occurred. Extending this principle, however, entails a reciprocity. If the *tremendum* interprets everything, the entire past lies under its mark. Nothing of the past can be omitted, neither suppressed nor described in such a way as to blunt its evidence. The whole of the past constitutes the environment of the modern Jew as the *tremendum* marks the fragmentation of his center. The rabbinic tradition obliges the center of modern Judaism, notwithstanding the conviction of many Jews that its determinations are antiquated, marginal, and irrelevant to the "modern" in modern Judaism. The belief of Christians that a Messiah is born out

of the people of Israel contends with the unfulfilled messianism of Israel, notwithstanding the conviction of Jews
that the claim of Christianity is self-deceiving and false. The
speculative inquiries of Judaism—revisionist theologies,
mystical teaching, counter-historiographies—submit to
question and doubt traditional formulations of the relation
of God, world, and man, notwithstanding the well-
established disinclination of contemporary Judaism to conduct theology, mysticism, or counter-history as serious disciplines of inquiry.

It is commonplace to defend the *status quo ante* in each
sector of the historical thrust by making appeal to the relative acceptability of another: the rabbinic tradition will be
upheld by some as a means of countering the thrust of
revisionist theology; or mystical epistemologies will be put
forward to engage the claim of Christian faith. In each
episode of self-defense, the boundary-sector of the Jewish
environment will be narrowed in order to relieve pressure
upon another flank. But all this, it strikes me, is a dialectical
strategy of evasion, refusing confrontation not by reason of
pusillanimity but because the center, out of which Judaism
speaks, has given way. It was no problem for rabbinic
Judaism to deny Jesus as the Christ; or for philosophy to
make clear its claim for seriousness before the assaults of
entrenched medieval rabbinism; or for seventeenth-century
Judaism to repel antinomian messianisms by the elaboration of spiritual beliefs coherent with traditional observance.
Judaism was once able to cope with its borders because the
center held.

If Jewish belief and practice is at the center of the Jewish
world, if Jews wish to clarify what is Jewish in the Jewish
world, and, finally, if Jews wish to extend the claim
(whether passively as paradigm or actively as witness) to the
whole of the world that is not Jewish, it is obligatory to
rethink the relations of the environment to the center, the

parameters of the Jewish experience to the field of consciousness that recognizes and enfolds them. Whether he
choose it or not, each Jew has a religious environment which
implicates his life in the life of his neighbor, his community
in the life of the community, his belief beside other believers. He may have nothing to say; he may assume no
stance. Nonetheless his presence implicates himself in the
life of others by the fact of being among them. How much
more so now when the environment—no longer separatist
and indifferent—implies his existence no less stringently
than he implies its own.

There are at least three constellations of nexus that express the Jew's relation to his religious environment: the
rabbinic tradition that asserts something definite about the
character of revelation received and transmitted; the contention of Christians that the Jesus of the Gospels is the
Christ of the Jews says something definite about the doctrine
of the Messiah and redemption; and the *tremendum* of this
century says something definite about the historical world
that grows from creation. All of these are mixed realities
that oblige the Jew to an ambivalence and incertitude coherent with their intrinsic ambiguity. Notwithstanding
their ambiguity, contemporary Jewish religious thinking
must have regard for the rabbinic view of the revealed word
(even if only to say no), the Christian view of salvation (even
if only to say no), the secular reading of history (even if only
to say no). The no, however simple, is a declaration of position that obliges defense and clarification, if only to insure
that the no be heard. The three form, therefore, more than
methodological limits. They are substantive orders in tension with which the exposition of the content of the
center—the authentic Jewish *noesis*—takes place. We can, in
short, know nothing as Jews unless we have dealt with the
environment that borders our life.

Surely, the traditional orthodox among Jews will argue

that the rabbinic corpus of law and teaching is not an environmental limit of Jewish reality but the reality itself. The traditional Christian will contend that the belief in Jesus as Christ is no environmental limit of Israel but the heart of salvation. The radical secular interpreter of the *tremendum* will fix the holocaust as the end of religious tradition beyond which there is no prospect of renewal. To my view, they must all be regarded as religious environmentalists because they point to the center of Jewish perplexity by indicating the extremity of its limits. I take boundaries as boundaries. What lies before me is the undertaking of making clearer what takes place within their confines. The rabbinic tradition is the distant visibility of the historical tradition, the Christian contention intermediate history, the *tremendum* near at hand. The *tremendum* contends with the rabbinic by contesting the ground of its theism; it contends with Christian faith, withering the promise of ransom and redemption, for martyrs are all saints, Dietrich Bonhoeffer or Karl Gerstein or six million Jews, but the slayers were all baptized, it contends with the stony cynicism of modernity that accepts its own judgment as being final.

The *tremendum* marks an end, but every end augurs a beginning. There is no end until the end is final. Until *that* moment, it is only caesura and new beginning.

· 3 ·

HISTORICAL THEOLOGY
AND THE TREMENDUM

Theology is the only intellectual discipline which by its very nature is inadequate. Its inadequacy does not arise from the ineptness of its formulation or the imprecision of its language or the insufficiency of the experience on which it is founded, but from all of these raised to the unlimited. Every other inquiry is certain of its subject matter and within the parameters set by its problem can, laboring patiently and over centuries, define acceptable solutions. These other disciplines may be obliged, over the course of time, to alter their schema and innovate procedures of encompassing and accounting for more of the content they aggrandize, but they remain confident that through the defects of earlier methodologies, newer complexities are disclosed and, grounded on the rectification of the inadequacies of earlier investigations, they gradually come to encompass more and more of their proper object.

Theology possesses no comparable optimism since it begins at the point at which all its relevant information is known and whatever it is likely to come to know is already before it, waiting without irony, to be discovered as if for the first time. God gives himself to theology that he may be known. God is discovered by philosophy that philosophy may be vindicated. Every other discipline of knowledge has

59

no need of God, although from time to time they may come upon him, a buried reality, like a newly discovered tomb, awaiting the ventilation of fresh air and novel theories to explain his odd incursion into the domains of biology, astrophysics, psychology, where he may be held accountable but of no essential account (for indeed, as God's role expands in the speculations of scientific cosmologists, for example, they become like theologians, while remaining ostensibly philosophers).

Theology, of course, is not indifferent to the knowledges around it. The knowledge of the world is the environment of theology, supplying it with findings and disclosures that enriched and increasingly precise inquiry into ordinary speech, ordinary experience, ordinary knowledge can impart. The natural and biological sciences, linguistics and semiotics, history, psychology, and the arts—pursued independently of the interests of theology—all supply their findings to the theological inquest. Theology hears everything, but such an abundance is not the source of its inadequacy. It is rather that the theological inquiry entails an almost paradoxical reversal, a tautology that is both its humility and its arrogance. The problem of theology is raised at the same time as its answer is supplied. The plight of every other human inquiry arises from the fact that its end is virtual in its premises; what it can conclude is hidden from the beginning in the morphology of its principles so that the great innovations of discovery lie not in the recasting of the goal but the redescription of the assumptions of beginning. Theology, however, is always the theologian's knowledge and the theologian does not set forth to find God, but having already found him seeks to formulate in accessible and unequivocal language what it is he has learned in faith (faith in such a reading being perhaps, as it should be at this juncture of the discussion, no more than religious code for intuition or Pascal's knowledge of the heart).

The theological procedure does not put the questions of philosophy as philosophic questions, since the philosopher raises himself up to belief only if the content of his knowledge remains under the sovereignty of mind. The philosopher dares not claim truth for more than he can reasonably explicate, and what he can reasonably explicate is bonded to the limits of mind and its language. The philosopher always falls back to the clarification of the self and the world, and the world that he designs is one over which his reason exerts sovereignty. Philosophy is modest in its arrogance, refuting or postulating a divinity under its control, that is to say, one limited by the fact that it is finite mind which describes its venture in the universe. It is hard now, more than a century later, to understand the enormous threat that Hegel posed to theology. We may be terrified by the posture of comprehensiveness, the definition of the bloodless schema or antitheses and synthesis, the optimism of integrating spiritual mind and historical energy, but now beyond the reach of Hegel's categories, we recognize that the individuality of the thinking, suffering, feeling person (whom Schelling, Kierkegaard, Rosenzweig wished to protect as the solitary knight of consciousness, spirit, freedom) has been beaten to his senses by other forces, not the least of which has been the *tremendum*.

Historical catastrophe ends certain intellectual options as surely and powerfully as it ends lives. The inadequacy of theology—the fact that its object can be formulated but never grasped, that its language approaches its object but can never exhaust it, that beyond every formulation of theological language the mystery of the living God remains—is warrant, however, for the theological heroism, that the theologian is given what he breaks himself to understand and what he comes to understand is only the shadow of the substance. The predicament of the theologian is that he is regarded by others as a thinker locked into a massive *petitio principii*, building an edifice to exemplify what is already revealed, to explicate what he already believes as certainty. But this, too, is part of mythologized opinion, the consensus of both true believers and nonbelievers holding that the theological inquiry is ultimately beside the point—either one believes, in which case theology is so much needless and obfuscating argument, or one does not believe, in which case theology is incapable of effecting persuasion. The mistaken assumption of both views is that theology is undertaken as an instrument of civil discourse, that its task is to develop a system of mediate principle which enables the experience of faith to become the reinforcing doctrine of the public weal. This is, of course, one of its employments. But more profoundly, I would suggest that theological method and language (no differently in this respect than philosophical method and language) are devised in order to render privacy accountable: to remove from the welter of private speech—where emotion, history, presupposition, the unconscious, the living passion of the human being has precedence—common terms, generalizable characteristics, transmissible judgments and form for them a language that opens each human being to the other, in time forging for them a community of shared gesture, symbol, expression, and ratiocination in which the struggle to speak truth about God and man is the highest goal.

II

It does not begin this way. The Erasmian vision of theology as a humanist discipline is early in the history of the West, but like many of the West's visions, it has been denied its victory.

The theologian is no spokesman for general belief but rather for the presupposition of his own revelation. He cannot, for example, speak for Christian faith until he has first become a Christian; he cannot claim for Judaism until he is first a Jew.

The Christian begins and the Jew is born. Beyond the definition of these limits, the work first commences. The believing Christian, the observing Jew are revealed into belief and in the afternoon of belief seek a discipline of language that enables them to enter the conversation in which belief is elaborated that it may be strengthened, refined that it may be purified of imprecision and confusion, etiolated that it may compass more and more of the human experience. The asseverations that both may be pressed to make about all belief are only generalizations beyond the premises of specific revelation. There is no such thing as general belief about the nature of God, world, and man. If there were an expressible identity between what theology could propose as general truth and the findings of any particular community of belief, either the particularity and nuance of revelation would disappear or else the mind would have achieved a facultative infinity that enabled it to arrive at probative truth independent of the groundwork of revelation.

All theology begins then with its own facts, in our case, with Jewish facts. The moment theology begins to speak, it speaks from its own sources, with a conditional sense of its history, with a knowledge of its traditional declarations, with command of its literary origins, within a community of grammatical and liturgical formulations that make plain the revealed provenance of its subject matter and its hermeneutics.

The difficulty of Jewish theology that has made all its undertakings vulnerable to attack stem, in my view, from a misunderstanding of what the theological inquiry undertakes. Jewish theological thinking has been regarded as a species of dubious argumentation, devised by uncertain belief to combat either militant unbelief or aggressive misprision.

In the ancient world, before the emergence of Christianity, the refusal of classic Judaism to enter into more than peripheral communication with its pagan environment and its philosophies derived from the conviction that there was no need for revelation to debate its merits with idolatry and polytheism. This may well be, however, a received interpretation because the rabbinic literature is not forthcoming with detailed description of the ideological combat of the rabbis with the Epicureans, Skeptics, Sophists. There is scant evidence of their formal exchange, other than for frequent reference in the rabbinic literature to conversation between pagans and Jews in the interest of clarifying a decretal of revelation, a point of ethics, a matter of jurisprudence. The Greek tradition is formulaically invoked, its hypostatic pagan or *epikoros* mentioned as exemplar of incomprehension or obstinacy or folly in the face of clear Jewish teaching. It may well be the case that the alien *epikoros* (generically, the denier, historically the Epicurean addict of time and pleasure) served a dialectical function to the clarification of Jewish practice no different functionally than the indigenous *'am ha-'arez*; the one, an instructed but pagan foreigner, the other, an uninstructed but Jewish peasant. Both avail a formulaic counter to the rabbinic voice, speaking familiar objection, asking naive question, providing the wisdoms of the good, but ignorant, heart or, in the case of the ardent pagan, the malign and distorted heart. The theological inquiry, as it came to be defined during the Middle Ages, was reflected in the classic tradition only by the elitist pretension of gnostic formulations that were oppository to halakhic polity because the gnostic adept (even if he was meticulously observant) was engaged in a study that he regarded as more pertinent and germane to his salvation than study of the Law. Indeed, then, it may well be the case that here in its origins an aspect of the historical Jewish opposition to theology has its ground, that theology has an exacting, unending, consuming interest in raising questions which it regards as prior and deeper than those of the Law. Moreover, if we accept the persuasive argument of the historian, Jacob Neusner, that in classical Judaism authentic Jewish theology was Mishnaic study and all rabbinic theologizing was thinking out of the ground of halakhic inquiry, raising only questions limned by the purview of its proper orders of study, clearly both original gnosticism and theological inquiry (tainted as methodological gnosticism) are suspect. To such a theology of Mishnaic study, the determinations of right reason and the establishment of coherent relations between orders of existence were everything. Those larger, ambitious, diffusive and seemingly anarchic inquiries that Greece devised to account for a universe without revelation were for the rabbis so many marks of their irrelevance or, worse, their danger. It was not, then, that the rabbis dared not combat the Greeks or feared their victory if the argument was joined, but rather believed them so circumstantial and irrelevant as to be beside the point of seriousness. Theology, understood as metaphysical philosophy, was either corrosive in its gnostic aspect or an impudent waste of time. This view survives to the present day.

After the emergence of Christianity and the incorporation into Christian argument of methods of analysis and exposition that depended upon the procedures of Greek philosophy, the refusal of Jewish thinking to argue acquired additional strength. Christianity, despite its rejection of Marcion's heresy, had nonetheless introduced into its reading of Hebrew scriptures a mode of differentiation that— even if it did not deny the Jewish God of Creation—made him into what Judaism could only consider a duplicitous and ambiguous revealer. To imagine, as Christian figurative exegesis of scripture insists, that the revelation of God contained a subterranean course of prophetic adumbration (that God used the kings and prophets as means of announcing the coming of Jesus Christ) not only had the effect of making God's revelation to Israel a complexity requiring an uncongenial typological analysis but cast doubt upon the conviction of the ongoing and continuing revelation of God to the community that survived the destruction of its Temple and now prayed and learned in order to express its covenant with God. Christianity argued the interruptive incarnation and resurrection with a people that believed itself to conserve the living word. The confrontation was hopeless as a contest of belief. It is no wonder that, during the centuries that followed, hopelessness of humane discourse was transferred to the social, political, and economic arena where power won the battle of ideas more efficiently than pacific debate.

By the Middle Ages, however, moved less by Christianity than by the rise of Islam—a community of belief that resembled Judaism as a printed page, laid over its manuscript model, touches its superfices but cannot be forced to synchronize or merge—Judaism began the work of exposition and interpretation, setting forth a doctrine that enabled belief to garner either universality or rationality, without sacrificing what is all along the indispensable idiom of its ontology, the definition and practice of the Law. When Christian disputation with medieval Judaism is recorded by Christians, as in the exemplary dialogues of Ramón Llull or Peter Abelard, the Jew is always construed as though he were a man with excellent civil practice and natural gift but inadequate grace, while for the Jew in similar disputation, the Christian is confuted by riddling his reading of Hebrew scripture with a version that exposes him to be the prisoner of a compromised divinity and a false messianism.

Although Jewish religious philosophy produced many and exceptional works prior to the eighteenth century, it did so at considerable risk. Within the Jewish community, the religious thinker was considered a man of heterodoxy and putative heresy who, only by the immense meticulousness of his observance or by the even more remarkable ability to produce works of halakhic interpretation side by side with compatible philosophy (Maimonides and Nahmanides are preeminent examples) could persuade his own community that he did not employ speculation as a means of straining or debilitating belief, but rather as an instrument of insuring its tensility and usefulness in apologetic polemics. Philosophy could be used to strengthen Jewish belief in a world where that belief was combated in a manner wholly different from the ancient world's annoyance with Jewish incivility or the modern world's use of religious language as a rhetoric to shore up the civil consensus of the predominantly secular society.

Until modern times, the Jewish philosophic enterprise was unavoidably linked either to the elaboration of a structure that led to the interpretation and grounding of the Law in a beneficent and providential God (the relation of Maimonides' *Sefer HaMada* to the systematic exposition of the *halakhah* that surrounds it in the *Mishneh Torah*) or else the God of the Jews is upheld as a given whose qualities and actions, whose benefactions and providence need only be displayed before the non-Jew to win his change of heart and conversion (the essentially fundamentalist declaration that enables the rabbi to vanquish his opponents in Jehudah Halevi's *Kuzari*). In the one, philosophic exposition is intended to complement revelation, for what Maimonides and his successors achieve is the elevation of speculative analysis to the level of revelation, making explicit what is all along taken for granted, namely, that the God who reveals Torah is a God of a specific nature. Religious philosophy has the limited function of making clear what is all along known, to explicate what is taken as the ground of action.

Maimonides as theologian is the explicator of divine mystery—mystery understood here, not as inexpressible *numen*, but as that which is unclear only because hitherto unclarified. Even where the discussion is moved beyond the metaphysical grounding of the Law in the decretals of divine polity (as in the *Sefer HaMada*) to the *Moreh Nebukhim (The Guide for the Perplexed)*, what occurs is a breaking open of the conclusive rubrics of the *Book of Knowledge (Sefer HaMada)* to an inspection that enables them to be defined before proponents of the Islamic *Kalam*. Since it would be pointless to argue to the Muslim (or the Christian for that matter) the merits of Torah and *halakhah,* since these constitute the paradigmatic revelation to the believing community and, as a result, a body of Jewish facts posterior to the assertion of a confessional belief, Maimonides undertook *The Guide for the Perplexed* to cut the theological discussion free of its devolution into law and to define a doctrine of religious knowledge coherent with Jewish experience, developing a theistic teaching that accords with all the findings and caveats of scripture, discriminating between the knowable and the unknown, the assertable and the unassertable, the inscrutable from the manifest deity. As the argument advances, the promise of metaphysics gives way to the argumentation of theology strictly speaking, the availability of information to all thinking men yields place to the description of the God who covenanted himself and revealed his ways to Israel, that it might become the instructor and guide to the nations.

Jehuda Halevi (1085–1141) works from a rather different order or preoccupation. As devotional or expository theology, essentially antimetaphysical and antirationalist at its heart, the *Kuzari* (whose full title in its Arabic original is *The Book of Argument and Proof in Defense of the Despised Faith*) has as its premise not the clarification of Judaism to the Jew or the explication of its ʾGod to those who have right belief but seek knowledge. Rather it is a work intended to speak to the non-Jew. Its dramatic occasion is the pagan king of the Russian Khazars who wishes to live a life exemplary and acceptable to God. The nature of God, the purview of his will and providence, the relation of his person to creation are all worked through as epiphenomena or acceptable acts. Halevi wishes to instruct action rather than intellect; his preoccupation is with giving grace and peace through obedience to Torah and *halakhah*.

Of course, the ultimate intent of both theological procedures is the same: whether the speculative philosophy of Maimonides or the moral-devotional theology of Halevi, both have the intention of causing Jew and pagan to learn the Torah and do the commandments. The *vita activa* is everything; the contemplative life, the devotional life, the reflective life all have as their objective that the believer live a life within Torah and its study, since life within Torah is not historical life but life eternal.

Traditional Jewish philosophy and theology had all but disappeared by the end of the eighteenth century. Without diagramming the history of the rise of the secular state and the emancipated intellect, it may be taken that the terms of religious inquiry had begun to alter by the time of Moses Mendelssohn and his descendants. The underlying issue had ceased to be one of belief gathering the resource of reason to strengthen and deepen faith or to preserve one's community against the aggression of the hegemony or even to give comfort to one's own world by the assertion of apologetic triumph, even if only among the remote Khazars. Secularism has been devious, a sinuosity that infects most virulently as the strain of its convictions weaken. It is a hard ideology to combat because it is no philosophic doctrine, but rather a dissolution of doctrine, a position that reflects more the instinctive movement of culture toward autonomous intelligence and will and heteronomous sectors of the public order where authority is immanent, validation empirical, values dialectical, goals historical and finite.

III

Jewish philosophy *out of* the tradition ended in the modern world. A sealed and sturdy community to whom it might speak, and whom its speculations served, had dissolved. The Jewish people was no longer univocal in subscription and communality. It remained bonded to the same Law, but henceforth a Law within the law of the civil polity. It has been said many times that the emancipation was a mixed blessing—mixed to be sure, but blessing nonetheless. Unless one's view is fundamentalist (and fundamentalism becomes more extreme and unyielding as its unexamined premises are stretched farther from their life in the homogenous community), the emergence of the Jewish people into the society of nations and peoples must be regarded as a benefice, if not now, then in the future, for the free service of God within the constraint of community can become one day the free community within the constraint of the critical imagination. However, during the two centuries that have elapsed since the struggle for emancipation began, Jewish religious thinking has ceased in great measure to be theological.

Jewish thinking has moved far from its original provenance, ceasing to be a mode of self-clarification and defense and becoming, as its intimacy and involvement with other peoples, cultures, and religions increased, an instrument of self-ennoblement and ingratiation. As Jewish thought began to concern itself with self-translation, it began to acquire a language of interpretation that pressed upon others a vision of its conditional and dependent excellence. In the will to become acceptable to the nations, Judaism developed a view of itself that established resemblances and correlations with them; but as its strategy of supplying such resemblances served to weaken the will of its own alienated constituency to remain strong within the historic community, it countered precisely such argument by claiming that the nations were at most pallid and frequently deformed representations of Jewish social ethics, prophetic teaching, and messianic vision. The first and most commonplace recognition of the intellectual compromise of Jewish thinking in the age of emancipation is the emergence of a religious anthropology stripped of theological grounding, although still dependent upon theological myth and symbol. We may point to at least four types of teaching that developed from the liberal pursuit of a nontheological reading of Jewish society:

a) The polity of the Jews is described as one grounded in revelation but, nonetheless, interpretable coherently with the findings of natural law and hence compatible with the requirements of the desacralized secular state (Moses Mendelssohn).

b) The situation of the Jew is set forth as one requiring a mimesis of the nations in their own unexceptionable need for soil and indigenous self-respect (Moses Hess, Max Nordau, Theodor Herzl).

c) The religious talent and social vision of prophetic Judaism is regarded as the inspiriting origin, in the case of Hermann Cohen, of enlightened Germany, and in the case of Mordecai M. Kaplan, of Anglo-American democracy.

d) A selective reading of classic Jewish sources defines a vision for the reconstruction of person and community in the West (Martin Buber).

Such religious anthropology providing a basis for asking the question of the nature of man, in the absence of being able to inquire any longer about the nature of God, matured, throughout the period of emancipation and enlightenment, a mediate doctrine which linked Judaism and secular culture without requiring that either be understood on their own terms. Both became functions of the other and, well employed, fulfilled the popular need for justification with its appropriate and useful ideology.

But Jewish philosophy, as well, reclaimed its voice during this era, reclaimed it in response, less to the demands of the proper issues of theology, than in aggravated reply to the erosion of Jewish belief and community: (a) the fundamentalist put on the habiliments of rational argument, setting forth the groundwork of a literalist reading of the tradition, believing that it was rehearsing the discourse of Maimonides without recognizing that were Maimonides writing in the nineteenth century, he would not have argued as did Samson Raphael Hirsch; or else (b) as did Ludwig Steinheim or Solomon Formstecher, accepting the challenge of Schleiermacher, addressed the problems of creation and revelation as critical centers of theological confusion; and by developing for the first time a nonmystical hermeneutics of the problem made naked their centrality to Jewish thinking, risking all the while that by making these problems central, they made them also exclusive, losing thereby the whole for the sake of the center; or (c) interpreting the problem of God as a problem that drove toward, but not through, the philosophic issue of internal relations, the excluded man or the excluded God, the God who is subject before the creature who objectifies, the creature who reifies in order to understand and loses the mystery and wonder that define both the limits and the possibility of God's existence. Such dialectical existentialism, immensely rich and suggestive, is finally undermined by the need to maintain the perpetual tension between God and man in which history extrudes structure and continuity for the sake of the spontaneous *ekstasis*. However much Martin Buber wanted to make such argument the ground of Judaism, it had the consequence of rendering it an aesthetic doctrine, because a Judaism of *Er-*

lebnis and spontaneity cannot be transmitted. And finally, (d) the religious philosophy of Franz Rosenzweig combined two methodologies into the single most constructive and fully expressed contest with the issues of classic Jewish theology and the demands of Jewish reality. Rosenzweig first identified, through the most painstaking phenomenological bracketing, the isolate and autonomous sectors of the real, cutting away the sureties of autonomous intellect and proceeding in a method that builds from technical and linguistic sources in Nicholas of Cusa and Giordano Bruno, Meister Eckhart and Jakob Boehme, Kant and Schelling, a generative-motor argument that compels each independent integer of the universe—God, world, man—to require each other, to set forth toward each other, to make contact and finally to become related to each other. The nexus of each integer to each describes a *meta-physis* within God, a *meta-logos* within the world, and a *meta-ethos* within man. These mediate, internal relations sufficient to philosophy are rendered by the transcending language of theology into creation, revelation, and redemption and translated into the paradigmatic Jewish and Christian communities of faith that press the holdings of belief into life.

IV

The project of Jewish thinking to the borders of the *tremendum* marks out an enterprise of clarifying the grounds for maintaining the internal durability of Jewish community and practice against the background of an environment of enmity. The relative intellectual vitality of medieval Judaism resulted from the fact that, in a world in which all men were obliged to have religion, the Jews possessed one which could be explicated and defended as the primordial text of their opponents. The function of Jewish religious philosophy was to supply the grounds in reason and nature for the polity of Israel and the function of theology was to provide interpretations of Jewish law. The confusions of conscience that occasionally brought medieval Jews to the borders of faithlessness and disbelief rarely resulted in their desertion of Jewish identity and practice. The mind wavered, faith was stunned, providence questioned, and to these Maimonides, for instance, replied, but in devising the *Mishneh Torah* his concern was the difficulty of mastering Jewish practice, reconciling apparently contradictory determinations in Jewish Law, affording an increasingly complex society with dependable guidelines to conduct.

All this had certainly vanished by the twentieth century. Jewish theology of practice had strained and fractured long before the *tremendum*. Jews were obliged by hostility to be conscious of their ethnicity, but now it was ethnicity and fragmented self-consciousness that brought Jews to the crisis of identity. The Jewish community before the *tremendum* was no longer analogous to Jewries of earlier centuries. Religious philosophy was no longer the companion of the study of Talmud; religious philosophy had become secular philosophy (in which religion was become a dimension of ethics and God the end-point of the metaphysical system) and theology had ceased to be the interpretation of the fixed grammar of Jewish life and had become, resembling Christianity in this (although treated in non-Christological format), the undertaking to devise a schema of thought at once metaphysically sound and religiously authentic (Hermann Cohen's *The Religion of Reason from the Sources of Judaism* as a heroic anachronism, reading scripture as a neo-Kantian document and Franz Rosenzweig's *The Star of Redemption*, a mystical epistemology that devolves into a classic aggadic reading of Jewish liturgy and Law).

The apparently invincible disengagement of Judaism from theology arises assuredly from the fact that Judaism does not conceive of itself as a body of received doctrine, formulated for intellectual transmission and defined for the reception and obedience of mind and will. Judaism does not regard itself as *docta*. The convenient exit of historical Judaism has been its insistence that it is an orthopraxy, discriminating itself by such usage from Christianity which it takes as orthodoxy. Orthopraxy is a miserable formulation, both ugly and inaccurate, sounding more like a branch of homeopathic medicine than religion. Like all such terms it is a shorthand, overstating a partial truth. Clearly, Judaism is a religion of enactment, specific acts and specific times, particular words conjoined to particular events. No less clearly, by rejecting those acts and words and commemorative events, a Jew debars himself from the concrete life of the Jew, cutting himself off from the community that either fulfulls the Law (believing it to be true because commanded by God) or accepts it as true evidence of Jewish communality, while insisting that its forms of enactment may be changed or altered, or else, in the extreme covenants of modernity, denies its origin in God, refusing its traditional enactment but still holding fast to the convocation of Israel that its ancient belief and enactment produced over the millennia.

The mythos of orthopraxy is self-fulfilling, for if Judaism is only a religion of enactment, then anything which describes itself as speculative reflection about Jewish acts is by definition irrelevant unless it is Jewish thinking about how more correctly, more precisely, more truly to perform Jewish acts. Jewish theology is then, as it has been, thinking about the Law and is merely a generally accessible nomenclature for describing the field work of the halakhist. What the Christian would call theology, the Jew calls philosophy—since there is no secular Jewish philosophy that is not by definition already beyond the boundaries of Judaism, concerned as such secular philosophy would be with the respects in which the Jew is not Jew but citizen of the state, socialist, humanitarian, pacifist, legist, etc., Jewish philosophy becomes, in such rendition, either a species of public language for secret teaching—as Maimonides indicated when he construed the *Moreh Nebukhim* as a teaching designed to disclose the supernal mysteries in the accessible language of the philosophic schools—or Jewish philosophy is the development of clusters of historical interpretation in conscious imitation of secular analogues—as Nahman Krochmal's incorporation of the Hegelian model—or it is a modality of effecting criticism of Jewish religious teaching, employing Kant, for example, to criticize the antiquated and superstitious teaching of Judaism (Solomon Maimon) or using Lessing and Kant's vision of the serene neutrality and good will of the public order as compatible with the alternate polity of Judaism (Moses Mendelssohn).

What is left to Jewish philosophy is either a critical role in the enhancement of Judaism in the eyes of those whose religion is belief, converting acts into principles, praxes into *docta*, that Judaism might become conversant with the nations, having mastered their language and forgotten its own, or else as an instrumentality of self-criticism and castigation or else as a screen methodology through which to transmit arcane doctrine in its publicly visible habiliments, a common enough practice when mystics speak as philosophers. But theology as I would understand it is the struggle to take account of an obdurate and unyielding field of contrariety, where the content of revelation is at odds with the evidence of history, where historical reality raises a fist against faith and smashes it—not simply acts and observances, not simply Law and practice, but the heart itself. This is, I grant, a new project for Jews, a new agenda for Judaism. The *tremendum* has smashed the presumptive self-declaration of secure orthopraxy; it has no less smashed Christian orthodoxy. I cannot address myself to the implication that the *tremendum* has for Christian theology, although I cannot believe that any Christian theology of a God *who has already saved* can make much sense after the *tremendum;* as well, the authorizing God who founded the Law through the giving of his name, that God in all his conventional providence and careful attention to the detail of the real, is no less impossible to Jewish thinking beyond the *tremendum.*

There has been little or no advance in historical Jewish theology after the Mishnah and the Talmud, but there is an implicit picture of the God who does his work through the Torah. That God, despite happy anthropomorphisms and intimacies, is construed as a God of immense distance and immaculate isolation, without qualities drafted from the observation of nature, bereft of any attributes of diminution or constraint, without limit and condition, without temporality and affect. A supreme and awesome integer of abstract grandeur and magnificence is our God. All Jewish thinking after the holy conversation of the *Tanaaim* is a theology of sanitization, a stripping away from God of every dimension that makes his felt presence in the arguments of the Law so deeply affecting. The act of Jewish learning as a mode of prayer and service is possible precisely because the mythos of the divine learner lies behind the devout student. How could such a life be ill spent or misrepresentative if God himself learns, if God himself guards the discussion of the sages, if God himself, invisible, participates in every liturgic event, of which study is principal. The presumptive theology of classic Judaism is of an endearing and gracious God who humbles himself to listen to his disciples and accounts their judgments right and true as consensus of Israel, even where he is importuned and minded to intervene. The incarnate God of study, the participatory divinity is, however, at loggerheads with the extreme monopolarity of Jewish theism. And it is with that monopolarity that we are left. The Jewish people is no longer a people of study, but a people who, without study and learning, are still led to the block of history. Such ironies and inversions. The people of ethnic purity and separateness, serving out the implication of their paradigmatic integrity, are led in the twentieth century, long after purity and ethnic integrity have ceased to be unquestioned values, to execution for being identifiably pure and integral. Secular history has learned the lesson of Jewish Law and executes us for it.

V

It is necessary to take up once again the argument set forth previously. If the *tremendum* marks off and separates; if it is caesura, how does one speak of God? God is, of course, in some sense, most immediately, presentness. He may be spoken of anew as if for the first time, our minds a *tabula rasa* from which the *tremendum* has erased memory and historical reflection. And surely this is not rhetorical formulation, although a methodological erasure of this magnitude is inevitably flawed by rhetoric. The force of the question is, however, that the *tremendum*, not alone as event of history, but as event that annihilates the past of hope and expectation confronts us as an abyss. As abyss, the *tremendum* transforms everything that went before into distance and remoteness, as though an earthquake had overturned the center of a world, obliterating mountains that had once been near at hand and that we had formerly dreamt of scaling. The *tremendum*, by definition, an ontological immensity, cuts through and parts our perception of the real and the principles we had inherited for its parsing and description. We can and do continue to perform old routines—like arms that instinctively reach out to grasp and hold although the hand has been severed—but we know that all is changed. The most optimistic and hopeful of peoples is certainly—despite the fantastic emergence of the Jewish State—a people of anxiety, confronting with nervousness the impingement of the great annihilation.

But what has all this to do with theology and thinking about God? Everything.

The *tremendum* as abysmal evil, as the ultimate negative historical configuration, is regarded by some as no less paradigm than the giving of Torah on Sinai. To make, however, the *tremendum* even the symbolic equivalent of Sinai is false. The claim of Sinai is that God spoke only to Israel, revealing his name to this one among the seventy nations of the world. But did the *tremendum* speak only to Jews? If only to the Jews then is all the rest of mankind exempted from hearing its meaning? If it is equivalent to Sinai as paradigm, intending that what the Jews heard on Sinai they should speak and witness to all the nations, a further disproportion is disclosed, for the people who attended at Sinai were addressed that they might hear and do, but the imperative of the *tremendum* is final solution for much more than Jews and Judaism. The unexpressed urgency of the symmetry of Sinai and the holocaust is that neither may be forgotten, that the indelible inscription of the one must be matched by the immemoriality of the other, the revelation at Sinai paralleled by the disclosure of the *tremendum*. But is the symmetry structural or polemical, real or hortatory? There are two responses that may be made: the first is that God's self-revelation at Sinai is not only ultimate *in our regard*, but ultimate in God's as well (everything that Sinai commands exhibits the involvement of God in the particularity of our lives—it is a measure of God's immanentism that his transcendence can speak its name to the people and evidence that it is he himself who speaks that name in thunder and in lightning), whereas everything that the holocaust reveals is ultimacy *in our regard* without the complementarity of God's authentication. Man speaks at and toward God in the *tremendum*, but God's voice is really silent (which is other than the implicit criticism so often made of God's silence at Auschwitz which entails a formal repudiation of his omnipotence and providence). The second response is that forming the symmetry of Sinai and the *tremendum* contradicts the *tremendum* as transforming caesura. If the holocaust is a monumentality structurally identical with or structurally complementary to or structurally indispensable as Sinai, it cannot be caesura. The one characteristic of the historical event as *tremendum* is that is annihilates for us the familiar categories by which we have read and decoded our past. The revelation at Sinai must be read differently after the *tremendum* because the *tremendum* disallows traditional memory, obliging it to regard all settled doctrine anew, all accepted principle afresh, all closed truths and revelations as open. Quite the contrary, therefore, the formulation must be that Sinai and the *tremendum* are nonsymmetrical, indeed, incommensurable and that our obligation to relate them follows not from their ontological resemblance or continuity, but from the extreme discontinuity that the *tremendum* inserts into Jewish history. We speak about them in the same breath because their relation is negative, the contrary of internality, sundering connection rather than effecting it. The only contact that Sinai and the *tremendum* make is the Jewish people.

The Jewish people is the reality that sustains both Sinai and holocaust. If the Jewish People is only of history (that is, if it has no God—and the silent God is treated by some of his critics as though speech were the only mark of affect or miracle the only modality of caring; hence silence is ineffectuality and the equivalent of the "not-God"), then Sinai and *tremendum* are shibboleths, for no amount of memorialization remembers and no amount of revelation persuades, the event at Sinai or at Auschwitz passing as history passes and memory fades. But if the Jewish people is an ontological structure, convoked and held in the maelstrom of immanence by the immeasurable concern of God, the matter comes out differently. One can slay God or declare the *tre-*

mendum a running amok, an historical "out-of-hand" which, like a madman's speech, has no truth to disclose other than about the nature of madness; but if one wishes meaning, structure is implied and if one wishes truth, each reality must be considered in itself and if one wishes interconnectedness, history cannot be the medium.

I take the view that to propose the symmetry of Sinai and the *tremendum* is an instance of overwhelming theological terrorization and evidence of a panic, so deeply felt, that its manifest coherence and consistency are taken as sufficient marks of truth. But coherence and consistency may be characteristic of obsessional disorder no less than of true perception. It is not that I could not bear to be persuaded that the solicitous God of Sinai is the malign God of the *tremendum,* and in convincing me, the love and compassion that I feel for God's lonely magnificence would die away within me, but to assert God's death in the interest of self-liberation seems to me a trifling narcissism and God's death only a memento of an already well-established irrelevance.

The irrelevance of God is, of course, a commonplace response of some modern thinkers not only to religion and its familiar forms but also to the apparent inadequacy of religious language and imagery to speak intelligently or clearly about the brutal facts of modern historical life. I have made the *tremendum* as crucial as I have precisely because it seems to me that the judgment upon traditional religious philosophy in Judaism and the theology of Torah reflect the considered opinion of the Jewish people that the classic tradition and the *tremendum* are not yet squared, that the traditional God has no connection with the holocaust despite the palpable fact that the immensity of the *tremendum* implies a judgment upon God. Jewish religious thinking that would seek, in a time as riven by ontic structures of evil as ours, the clarification of conceptual language in order to make its form and content coherent with advanced formulations of linguistic theory, philosophic analysis, and phenomenological hermeneutics, without reopening consideration of its fundamental theological presuppositions, is idle, cowardly, finally worthless.

The challenge of the *tremendum* to Judaism is not that traditional Jewish reality cannot survive the scrutiny of its teaching, that it will be found archaic or outmoded, that its inherited custom is insupportable, but rather that its view of its own depths will be found shallow, insufficiently deep and flexible enough to compass and contain the *tremendum*. Jewish reality must account for the *tremendum* in its view of God, world, and man; it must constellate Jewish facts of practice and belief in such a way as to enable them to endure meaningfully in a universe that endures the *tremendum* and withstands it and a God who creates a universe in which such destructiveness occurs. If either side goes, the whole collapses. If such a universe cannot withstand the *tremendum*, then it is not only ultimate but final. If God is creator of the *tremendum* he cannot be accounted good as classical theism requires.

VI

It is time now to build a bridge over the abyss of the *tremendum*. It is a bridge that spans the abyss but does not obscure it. Wayfarers upon the bridge, however its moorings in the past of the Jewish people and its future in the prospect of its ongoing life, cannot neglect the obligation to look over into the chasm beneath. They know the abyss but, since they pass along the bridge, they know equally that they do not have their being in its depths; however much the ineffaceable abyss informs them, their own being and proper life is elsewhere—on the bridge, in fact, over the abyss.

· 4 ·

THE BRIDGE OVER THE ABYSS
Schemas of Construction

The *tremendum*, as an ontological gathering of evil, is a watershed reality that casts doubt upon the formulations of traditional Jewish theism and requires, if it is not to be final as well as ultimate, a response in its aftermath that takes account of the profound challenge of its negativity.

I have tried, in what has preceded, to make clear the theological relevance of the holocaustal caesura. As well, I have undertaken a brief account of historical theology as it worked through the materials of traditional theism up to the borders of the holocaust, indicating something of its argument and difficulties. By the time of the *tremendum* of this century, the suppositions of classical theism had already passed through the testing fires of radical criticism that left them depleted. Only by recourse to a precipitous rush to mystery could the assertion of an absolute and monarchic God, whose relations to creation were at best formal and external, be reconciled with the scriptural disclosure of a loving, merciful, and just God. The God of classical theism, in no way constituted by his creatures or affected by the trials and alarums of creation, has disappeared finally into the folds of mystery, where reason cannot make meaningful the relativity implicit in God's involvement with creation and faith cannot make cogent the remoteness and impassivity that God's absoluteness requires.

The *tremendum* forces a resolution of this conflict, not alone as an obligation placed upon reason to account for its occurrence in a universe fashioned by a presumptively omnipotent, omniscient, and providential ruler, but even more as an obligation it places upon our humanity—as creatures without presuppositions—to account for the *tremendum*, to justify and redeem, if that is possible, the surpassing suffering of its victims and the unbearable guilt of its perpetrators. This is nothing more nor less than our obligation to account for the reality of God in the aftermath of the *tremendum*. The task entails (beyond the work of constructive theology that makes clear and meaningful the nature of God and his relation to the historical *scenum*) the translation of that constructive language into terms that will renew the meaning of creation and authenticate—as more than this century's groans for liberation—the promise of redemption.

I

What I undertake—and perforce within the abbreviated compass of this discussion it must be schematic—is a redefinition of the reality of God and his relations to the world and man, but as well a reinvestment of the passive receptiveness of the world and the active freedom of man with significant meaning.

The thinker has no choice but to stand precariously within his own limitation when he tries to speak, without subjectivity, about the nature of God and to stand firmly in his own freedom when he tries to speak, without detachment, about the actions of man in history. He must hold firmly to his freedom when he addresses the absolute God. But no less, when he describes the God of creation and redemption, he must contain the certitude of God's comprehensive perfection. It is a dialectical precariousness in which the absolutely existent (that abstract ground of all), remote and distant, parsed in the classical tradition by negative arguments that winnowed divinity of all admixture, is commingled with the divine concrete and caring, the presentness and immediacy that validates our own human individuality, the particularity of our destiny, and the futurity of our personal history.

The philosophic critique of classical theism (its insistence upon the irreconcilability of a God of absolute monopolarity and the scriptural evocation of an engaged and available God) obliged neo-orthodox theologians of earlier decades of this century to center the debate upon a different terrain. The God of medieval philosophy, sequestered within his forbidden supremacy, was bespoken in our world by a series of paradoxical formulations which guaranteed his absoluteness while assuring us of our freedom. The neo-orthodox formulations to which among Jews, Abraham Joshua Heschel and Will Herberg, with varying degrees of emphasis and assent, gave themselves, will blunt the epistemological inquiry by grounding the recognition of God as the preeminent object of wonder and the existential situation of the believer as one of faithful transcendence of philosophic question to trust in the generosity of the divine person. The negative theology of medieval Judaism gave way to assertions of paradox, too quickly passing from the difficulties of formulating cogent theology to the positing of ultimate mystery.

The varieties of neo-orthodoxy (and I suppose my own work prior to recent years would be classifiable among them) have had the effect of making the *tremendum* an event alongside historical events, neither of history nor of teleology, and hence beside the point of theological labor. Neo-orthodoxy does not cope adequately since it situates the *tre-*

mendum as the dialectic counter of an absent or hidden God, enabling the immensity of the one to pass the mystery of the other in the dark night of this century without compelling them to their dreadful confrontation.

Any constructive theology after the *tremendum* must be marked by the following characteristics: first, the God who is affirmed must abide in a universe whose human history is scarred by genuine evil without making the evil empty or illusory nor disallowing the real presence of God before, even if not within, history; second, the relation of God to creation and its creatures, including, as both now include, demonic structure and unredeemable events, must be seen, nonetheless, as meaningful and valuable despite the fact that the justification that God's presence renders to the worthwhileness of life and struggle is now intensified and anguished by the contrast and opposition that evil supplies; third, the reality of God in his selfhood and person can no longer be isolated, other than as a strategy of clarification, from God's real involvement with the life of creation. Were any of these characteristics to be denied or, worse, proved untrue and unneeded, as strict and unyielding orthodox theism appears to require, creation disappears as fact into mere metaphor or, in the face of an obdurate and ineffaceable reality such as the *tremendum*, God ceases to be more than a metaphor for the inexplicable.

The *tremendum* as ultimate oppository immensity obliges us to bring together two vectors of modern theological thinking, to join them by compelling their formulation in complementarity. There is, on the one side, the view enforced by Gershom Scholem's reading of the kabbalistic counter-history of Judaism that God, in the immensity of his being, was trapped by both its absoluteness and necessity into a constriction of utter passivity which would have excluded both the means in will and the reality in act of the creation. Only by the spark of nonbeing (the interior apposition of being, the contradiction of being, the premise of otherhood, the void that is not vacuous) was the being of God enlivened and vivified. Within such a cosmogonic mythology of a divine complex, gestational stages are described whereby God focused the nexus of nonbeing and being, withdrawing from nonbeing within himself to extrude nature from the void. The cosmogony of the Kabbalah entails scaled emissions of being which derive their nature and vitality from divine nature and life, emerging from lowest to highest, linked by the complexity of their own structure to the divine structure, by their own simplicity to the divine univocality, imperfect according to the portion of waste within the divine contraction, perfect according to the formal adhesion to the divine image.

This cosmogonic tradition, abhorred by historical Judaism for its seeming concession to the power of gnostic imagery, its no less palpable irrationality and mythic imagery, its involvement with neo-Platonic and later Christian emanationist doctrines, its devolution into magical and heterodox practice, has preserved its life as a hermetic teaching which, precisely because its texts were not critically edited, its canonic scholarship inchoate, its anti-modernism apparent, its fancifulness and obscurity part of its intellectual charm, has not emerged to light until the present day. It has come now to the forefront not least because of Scholem's superlative advocacy, but surely more because the times require it, calling forth from other quarters and persuasions considerations that demand revisionism since they, too, cannot abide the formulations of inherited orthodoxy.

The tradition cannot deal with the *tremendum* as it is presently understood, but the cosmogonic imagination of the Kabbalah does define a trope that indeed addresses it and can compass its oppository immensity. No less than the Kabbalah is a tradition of Western thought—heartily Christian in its auspices, but gnostic-kabbalistic in its origins, a tradition that runs from Joachim of Fiore through Schelling to Franz Rosenzweig. Briefly summarized, it is an interpretation that takes the formulation of the Johannine Gospel as metaphysical instruction and meditates its significance.

"In the beginning was the Word." The divine word is the origin of the creation out of the void (which, although empty, is not nothing; put more precisely, is Nothingness, although not nothing). The Gospel according to John opens with a gloss of the original assertion of the Book of Genesis: "In the beginning God created heaven and earth." Clearly not with hands, as a craftsman or master-builder, did God make the heavens and the earth. But as absolute and necessarily existent being, classic theism affirms.

The only instrument of creation, dephysicalized—the breath of being—is speech. The divine being speaks and creates. So much for the creation. The tradition of transcendental idealism that has its origins in Joachim's typological correspondences of the ages of the Church and the persons of the Trinity and Nicholas of Cusa's mathematical correlation of the minima of the world with the maxima of the creator through Jakob Boehme's mysticism of the plenteous nothingness of God's supernal ground to the Schellingian doctrine of the indispensable and informing contradiction—all these supply the logical trope of Franz Rosenzweig's *The Star of Redemption*. Schelling and Rosenzweig concur out of their sources that within God and before creation there is the working out of the parts of divine speech. The divine speech-grille, or rules of divine language, is not to be taken as only a metaphor for the anthropomorphism of divine speech. Obviously, it was easier to say that "God made" than that "God spoke." The creation that follows from the ambiguous making could retain its abstractness, pressed by negative theology, back to the fashioning out of nothing that need not speak its means. The

Gospel was for Hebrew ears a corrupt anthropomorphism, for the Psalmist contradicts the idolatrous imputation of divine speech, hearing, smell, handling; but the issue is not speech as such, but *logos* and *onoma* (name and language) which in Stoic teaching are linked as the interior archetype and its external formation. Philo of Alexandria is, of course, close to the Gospel in his use of *logos*, but for us the issue is not one of tracing historical proof-citations, but rather the suggestibility of certain conceptions of the creation.

Logos and speech are signs that direct us to aspects of God that may offer a way out of the dilemma of the absolute and necessary existent who is God and the miraculous fiat of *creatio ex nihilo*, by using the image of speech to describe a movement within God that occurs in his eternal instant and in our time for everlasting. The varieties by which Schelling describes this turning inwards within God, whose consequence is the turning outwards of creation, are, as Jehudah Halevi remarked, apparently complex because they are so simple. Most briefly described, Schelling's argument may be summarized in this way: "What is necessary in God," Schelling begins, "is God's nature," his "own-ness." Love—that antithetic energy of the universe—negates "own-ness" for love cannot exist without the other, indeed, according to its nature as love, it must deny itself that the other might be (contracting itself that the other might be, setting limits to itself). However, since the divine nature as *esse* cannot have personality without the outpouring, the self-giving of love to define those limits, it must be postulated that within God are two directions (not principles, as Schelling says): one which is necessary selfhood, interiority, self-containment and another, vital, electric, spontaneous that is divine *posse*, the abundant and overflowing. There arises from all this the dialectic of necessity and freedom, the enmeshment of divine egoity and person, divine self-love and free love, divine narcissism and the created image, the sufficient nothing of the world and the creation of being. The human affect is toward the overflowing, the loving in God; his containment, however, the abyss of his nature, is as crucial as is his abundance and plenitude. These are the fundamental antitheses of the divine essence without which the abyss would be unknown or all else would be regarded as plenitude. Another means of imagining this dialectic is through that of language and silence (the logos of revelation), for clearly the quiet God is as indispensable as the revealing God, the abyss as much as the plenitude, the constrained, self-contained, deep divinity as the plenteous and generous.

This is as perfunctory as I would dare to make the speculation of Schelling in *The Ages of the World* and book one of Rosenzweig's *The Star of Redemption*, which is built upon its foundations. Both together, Schelling for Johannine Christianity and Rosenzweig for the Jews, suggest the foundation of revisionist theism. Both share a common vision that only by assuming that human natures are created and, therefore, in reality dependent upon the operative analogue of divine nature can statements be made about the nature of human and divine life. Both would argue that only when we transcend our natural categories, mired as they are in finitude and limitation, extending the lines of the creative process, refining them of gross physicalities and pantheistic dependency, rendering them truly abstract because absolute and not abstract for the sake of absoluteness, is it possible to understand why creation follows from God as *his event of speech and love* rather than as an event mysteriously unfathomable and unaccountable. As God's being is full and plenteous, creation is an overflowing—the cosmogonic reading. As God's nature is abundant, what is plenitude for God is seen by his creatures as love—a religio-ethical reading. As the whole of the divine nature is enlarged by the presence of nonbeing, by the depths of the divine made manifest, so creation is necessity within God and free act to man.

The divine essence is dipolar in its nature and in its manifestation: movement within God is the premise of his nature and the plenitude of God (the manifold richness of his essence) is devised by us as the variousness of creation. Creation is already the gloss of wonder that makes the silent speech of plenitude vocal, naming it as creation without naming God, determining its irradiance without the sureness to confirm its origin. The divine nature eo ipso always overflows, that is, always creates, for the world is from the standpoint of the divine nature always in the beginning, never at its end. To be finished and concluded, to regard seven days literally, is mythic incapsulation that we employ as finite creatures (metaphysical language conserved as liturgical language), six days work and Sabbath rest are devices of symbolization that recall a metaphysical description that is in turn time-language recalling the divine word (all that was heard) that is for everlasting the beginning in God's eternity.

If what is absolute in God (that his nature is necessarily existent) is seen by us under the aspect of his plenitude, it must be said that God's relation to himself is different from God's relation to us; or, put otherwise, if the divine essence is the form of perfection and the divine egress from self and entrance into creation is the multifariousness of his potential for the creation of form, it would follow that God does not renew the work of creation daily, but rather that each day we acknowledge what passes ceaselessly within God, namely, that *our novelty* is a rehearsal of God's eternal plenitude. New forms, new beginnings, new creation for us are forms already within God, creations already predicated of God's armory of possibility, beginnings eternally begun within God. The dipolar God—the God of absolute being and internal involvement with the created—must be paralleled by bipolar vision, that we draw distinctions but maintain them in synchronicity, recognizing the difference between essence and creation, between Being and being, between the absolute rest of God and the engagement of his plenitude, between his eternity and his "in the beginning."

The world that the word made is silent for its logos has no throat. Within plastic nature, the freedom of God's interior negation elaborates the formal configurations of *physis* or nature—their drama of attraction and repulsion, charge and static field, penetration and seeming void. The world is the divine *scenum*, the mime theater where only the passivity of God's essence is displayed, hum of growth according to law, instinct, numb order, every irregularity altering the inadequacy of old formulations, demanding newer and more comprehensive readings, endlessly complex and ramified in its panoply, but in its essence as simple and monologic as silence itself.

The world (which is the passivity of God) is complemented by man whose essential character is freedom. It is not reason that makes man little lower than angels, but freedom and speech. Reason is facultative necessity, not unlike the passive necessity of God's nature which moves along the tried ridges and grooves of his unchallenged being. It is freedom, however, and the linguistic imagination that marks the attraction of nonbeing for the rationality of man. The implosion of the divine nature which, in its act, is devised as creation is no less recognized in our own existentiality. Man is a creature whose freedom tempts his reason. Otherwise formulated out of Schelling, nonbeing has in freedom the contradiction of being, for freedom is naked caprice before it is measured and bounded by the rational aspect of our being. There is in man an enduring strife and tension, enlarged and made threatening by our finitude, in which freedom enhances when it is marked and contained by reason, but when reason fails to find language, freedom is destructively cut loose or bends toward untruth or succumbs to sheer willfulness.

Reason orders the energy of caprice into freedom; being sets limits to the surge of nonbeing. Man reconciles and contains his contradiction, repressing madness and evil. This is the optimism and hope of being created in the image of God: his plenitude is always in the beginning of our ends and our true end—that God describes the limits but man sets them, that God engenders possibility but that man enacts them, that God's freedom to be eternally open to his own nature is our freedom to speak and enact in time.

We had thought at the conclusion of the nineteenth century that reason and universal telos had become one, that a single mind and energy ordered the universe, that reason was abundant, that progress and enlightenment represented the best and most beneficent humanizing of the races of mankind. Our innocence was deceptive and our trust naive or deceitful. The age was withered by the criticism of Marx who discerned the corrupt self-interest of institutions and the conversion of free energy into instrumental and manipulated power. Freud, no less a critic of the age, projected a pessimism of the limitless caprice and the insatiable id that was either to be chastened by the superego with the guilt of bonded service or else chastised in the hope of containing its limitless ambition. The Marxist critique devolved beyond the *tremendum* to an analysis of secular messianism that reintroduces hope as the measure and containment of social disruption. Post-Freudian critics are ready to recognize that Freud's attack on mythological religion was more an attack on unsuccessful repression than a debunking of the humanizing function of the sacred. Indeed, from the vanguard of the most radical opponents of historical religion may come forth interpreters who make vital again the essential appeal of a transcendent claim. Both Marx and Freud were prophets who have not been adequately heard. The machinery of society enlarged and reason withdrew, the dreams of disorder became habitual and the tyrannic machinery of repression failed. By 1945 the old world of hope was crushed forever and what stood forth, isolate, marked by grim parameters and horrendous reminders, never to be effaced as dreams become nightmares, was the *tremendum* of this century.

The bridge that I have, not casually but I fear insubstantially, cast over the abyss is one that sinks its pylons into the deep soil of human freedom and rationality, recognizing no less candidly now than before that freedom without the containment of reason returns to caprice and reason without the imagination of freedom is supineness and passivity. Since all of our world here below is marked by coming to be and passing away, birth and death, all human projects toward the world and its settlement are traded off against the selfishness of our preoccupation with our own finality. To engage man beyond the self, to win his free reason and his reasonable freedom requires beyond the life of the single man the containment of his community, where the freedom of all is open to the prophetic recall of the one. The life of man through God, both as imitation and as real presentation, is not surety enough unless enacted within community, where not only numbers maintain guard but also where collective language makes audible the silent speech of creation.

What the single man of being and nonbeing, passivity and affirmation, reason and caprice assembles as the creature of instructed freedom is, before the plenitude of God's engagement to the world, as silent in his gratitude as God is silent in creation. The word of God is God's flesh. It is only when man begins to speak that he enfleshes the forms of creation, naming their substantiality, devising their discrimination and identity, denominating their selfhood. Human grammar is divine, but divine speech is human. Or otherwise affirmed, what creation is for God is revelation for man, the silence of God becoming the speech of man. When God is denied, nothing can be named; when God is speculated, God remains the Something sought whose name is unknown; when God is affirmed the name of God is given; and when life is lived in community with God, God's name is spoken as continuous presentness, the ongoing *koh 'amar* ("Thus says the Lord") of creation answered by the response of revelation, *hinneni* ("Here I am").

II

The *tremendum* remains *tremendum*, neither diminished nor explained, but nonetheless limned by interpretation. As I have proposed, it has at least one interpretation that allows the enterprise of human community to endure, that encourages human struggle to persevere, that obliges trust to assert once again its claim upon the future. If the *tremendum* of evil was the dissolution of the fragile human integration of energetic caprice and orderly reason, the union of nonbeing and being, and, as if by some monstrous reversal, the structure of being was dislocated, order rather than reason machining caprice and the energy of caprice immolating reason, it is no wonder that the searing fire of holocaust would burn out Europe. How such a reversal of integration, such a dissolution of structure occurred, how the historical explosion was prepared is work enough for a century of historians, psychologists, and memorialists.

The *cri de coeur* of the memorialists of the *tremendum* is the silence of God. How could it be that God witnessed the holocaust and remained silent, that within the providential plan of God the holocaust should figure among its details, that God is vaunted presentness but was absent, that God is highest manifest reality but recondite and hidden. What, in truth, does the cry contend and require? Nothing less than the interruptive miracle, that the sea open and the army of the enemy be consumed? This is surely what all of us might have dreamt for the miracle of ransom. The ancient model, embedded as the scheme of our redemption from the land of

Egypt, is the prefiguration of modern hope. The interruptive God, however, is not ever interruptive even were the sea to part and close or the earth of Auschwitz to open and the murderers to fall in. The presupposition upon which such a view of divine miracle depends is that the creation we take to be real is not an emergence beyond God's being. Such a view of the miracle—to be coherent—must assert either that the created world is never independent of God, that it is, at most, the extension of God and that what appears as God's interruption is the logical trope of his own reflexivity. Such a pantheism, retracing its ground in Spinoza, makes suffering and evil unclarity and inadequate perception; or else, if not pantheism, it must return to the naive grounds of fundamentalist theism that considers God respondent to extremity, the greater the human need the greater the certainty of his assistance, with the result that human life denies its essential freedom, returning to ethical passivity and quietism in which everything is compelled to be God's direct work.

The most penetrating of post-*tremendum* assaults upon God has been the attack upon divine silence. Silence is surely in such a usage a metaphor for inaction: passivity, affectlessness, indeed, at its worst and most extreme, indifference and ultimate malignity. Only a malign God would be silent when speech would terrify and stay the fall of the uplifted arm. And if God spoke once (or many times as scripture avers), why has he not spoken since? What is it with a God who speaks only to the ears of the earliest and the oldest and for millennia thereafter keeps silence and speaks not. In all this there is concealed a variety of assumptions about the nature and efficacy of divine speech that needs to be examined. The first is that the divine speech of old is to be construed literally, that is, God actually spoke in the language of man, adapting speech to the styles of the Patriarchs and the Prophets, and was heard speaking and was transmitted as having spoken. God's speech was accompanied by the racket of the heavens so that even if the speech was not heard by more than the prophetic ear, the marks and signals of divine immensity were observed. As well, there is the interpretive conviction that God's speech is action, that God's words act. Lastly, and most relevantly to the matter before us, God's speech enacts and therefore confutes the projects of murderers and tyrants—he saves Israel, he ransoms Jews, he is forbearing and loving. God's speech is thus consequential to the historical cause of justice and mercy. Evidently, then, divine silence is reproof and punishment, the reversal of his works of speech, and hence God's silence is divine acquiescence in the work of murder and destruction.

Can it not be argued no less persuasively that what is taken as God's speech is really always man's hearing, that God is not the strategist of our particularities or of our historical condition, but rather the mystery of our futurity, always our *posse*, never our acts. If we can begin to see God less as the interferer whose insertion is welcome (when it accords with our needs) and more as the immensity whose reality is our prefiguration, whose speech and silence are metaphors for our language and distortion, whose plenitude and unfolding are the hope of our futurity, we shall have won a sense of God whom we may love and honor, but whom we no longer fear and from whom we no longer demand.

III

God and the life of God exist neither in conjunction with nor disjunction from the historical, but rather in continuous community and nexus. God is neither a function nor a cause of the historical nor wholly other and indifferent to the historical. I understand divine life to be rather a filament within the historical, but never the filament that we can identify and ignite according to our requirements, for in this and all other respects God remains God. As filament, the divine element of the historical is a precarious conductor always intimately linked to the historical—its presence securing the implicative and exponential significance of the historical—and always separate from it, since the historical is the domain of human freedom. Given these assumptions, it would follow that the *tremendum* does not alter the relation of God to himself, nor the relation in which God exists to the historical, nor the reality of creation to the process of eternal beginning within God, but it does mean that man—not God—renders the filament of the divine incandescent or burns it out. There is, in the dialectic of man and God amid history, the indispensable recognition that man can obscure, eclipse, burn out the divine filament, grounding its natural movement of transcendence by a sufficient and oppository chthonic subscension. It is this which is meant by the abyss of the historical, the demonic, the *tremendum*.

There is an insistence within classical Judaism that is instructive to this point. It is often noted, at critical junctures in Talmudic discussions of the Law, that God's interruptive sign might settle a given dispute; however, in each instance—even in cases where the divine sign is magically induced and the *bat kol* (prophetic voice) is heard—the settlement is made according to the findings of reason. It is not the case that the divine insinuation is ignored, but rather declared to be irrelevant. The ground of the dismissal is that the logic of the Law is now conserved by man, but not man pitted in his caprice against the interruptive sign, but man enlightened by revelation and the grammar of its unfolding. In short, freedom within history is the continuation of creation made articulate by revelation. *Halakhah*, in such a view, is the ongoing elaboration of the implications of revelation; its consignment to the deliberations of Jewish minds is recognition that freedom is the divine-human nexus, the containment of caprice and blind necessity is man's imitation of God, and the antimiraculous pursuit of the holy consensus is the way in which Jewish community works out its destiny.

The sacred consensus unfolds within the community of Israel as an ongoing exploration of revelation, requiring no further miracle, for every day is the miracle of renewed freedom.

There is an observation in the unpublished diaries of Franz Rosenzweig that is germane to this phase of my exposition. Rosenzweig writes on 11 July 1914:

> Judaism as well as Christianity is *un*systematic. But the difference rests in the Christian's appearing only as fact, the Jew's as theory (Torah). In Christianity the significance of the fact, revelation, has therefore to be fitted into a complete philosophical system (Christology): analogous experiments signify mysticism to us; our legitimate method may not proceed from the fact (the people) but only from history. The Torah, however, although theory, is no system. It can therefore *not* result in a system of Judaism as there are systems of Christianity, but it might be dissolved into verifications, respectively opposing arguments, to lead to the philosophical system—the philosophical system has to remain as it is since the Torah has neither systematic force to incorporate it nor can it be incorporated as fact to enable it to become Jewish from within.*

My comment upon this passage is that the incarnation of God in Jesus of Nazareth is revelation, however the divinity revealed is mutant divinity. It is no longer God; it is not wholly man. The meeting place is no longer world. That is to

---

* This extract from manuscript page ZZ 3 of the translation of Franz Rosenzweig's diaries made by Jehuda Reinharz in 1973 has been transcribed from my copy of the Reinharz translation. I have no doubt of its accuracy since it has that gnomic simplicity which all of Rosenzweig's journal notations possess.

say, the revelation has to be accounted for by Christology, by a *noesis* of the Christ. The revelation, instead of merely shattering the composure of unbelief or the trial of belief, becomes the object of epistemology. Hence the illusion of the system. But in Judaism, where there is no incarnation, there is still Torah. There is thus the gift of revelation that does not compromise either the giver, the receiver, or the place of its giving in the world.

Torah is an *objectivum*, the sealed book of the word that would remain *objectivum* until the hearing man engages the speech-grille of God from which the open and legible book of revelation proceeds. The Torah is *as such*, but not as mediation or incarnation. Torah is then a *teoria* more than it is a praxis. Those who think Judaism a praxis—a web of deeds and enactments—have to rethink here. Praxis is not revealed; praxis is empirical conformance to the model. Torah is model—*teoria*—a nexus of conformance between the modalities of divine egoity and the human person. Torah is not a system because it does not proceed from a visible fact—the people—nor is it, as in Christianity, the attestation of the presence of a Christ in Jesus of Nazareth. In short, the Torah is a schema of revelation, schema being significantly different than system. There are different schemas of Judaism but not different systems, because for no one among the schemas is it possible to deny Torah as revealed *teoria*. *Teoria*, however, requires confirmation and the variant forms of Jewish practice and institutional organization are variant systems of confirmation. The *teoria* is confirmed and adapted by the different praxes, but is not modified thereby as revelation.

IV

It is an unresolved predicament of Jewish thought to speak correctly about the relationship of the Jew to history, the Jewish people to the nations, the eternal vortex into which

God inserted Torah and the inescapable obligation of the Jew to be citizen among citizens and neighbor to neighbor. Where the argument has formed itself by constrasting the community of the Jewish people to the hegemonies of the world, once Christian and Muslim, now Christian, Muslim, and socialist, as well, the position of the Jew was dialectically neutralized, but only in the dialectic, for the Jewish people has now taken up the arms of the world to stand before the world. But if the Jewish people takes up the arms of the world before the world, its reality is for the first time measured against the ominous magnitude of the world, its resolute independence becomes its isolation, its active refusal of the world's monocular conception of the Jew as history's outsider is now contested by the world's numbers before the numerical smallness of the Jewish people. It may well be the case that the full entrance of the Jewish people into the lists of the historical is more threatening even than genocide has been, for in no way is the Jew allowed any longer to retire to the wings of history, to repeat his exile amid the nations, to disperse himself once again in order to survive. One perceives that when history endangers it cannot be mitigated. This we know certainly from the *tremendum*, but we know it no less from the auguries of nationhood, that every structure of history in which an eternal people takes refuge is ominous. Time is always shortsighted and partial; yet its power (for those to whom time-victories are all that matters in a world where eternity is denied prefigurement in revelation) is as final as though there were no eternity and no revelation. History without a capstone, time without eternity, the present moment without the inbreeding of the *eschaton* leave us, as Jews, with little more than the chthonic vitalities of our blood as shield and buckler.

This is the premise of the predicament, that returned to history out of the millennia of the ahistorical where Judaism

carried on its single meta-historical task of saying no to
idolatry and latterly to Christianity and Islam, reflecting in
the mirror of the historical the single image of its attentive-
ness and impassivity, the Jew has returned out of the ashes
of the *tremendum* to the historical *as an historical agent.*

This is something that was in no way anticipated by
Jewish thinking prior to these decades. The solemn grandeur of Franz Rosenzweig's teaching and the riveted intensity of Martin Buber's prophetism derived their power in
considerable measure from the fact that for Rosenzweig history was always a construction, through whose mesh the
living stream of revelation could be pressed, and for Buber
the historical was never (as Reinhold Niebuhr correctly
noted) the context of real structures and powers, but always
distortions of primary relations. History was for both thinkers scaled-down and diminished scorings of the immense
Hosanna toward which time irresistibly moved, gathering
in the gale of revelation the winds of God's force which
would one day—now, tomorrow, in the distant future—of a
sudden, become the end-point of the Kingdom. History was
not chimeric, not unreal, not irrelevant, not fanciful, but it
was also not the threshing floor of man and God. It was as
Rosenzweig called it the domain of the *Zwischenreich*—time
around the Kingdom, the buffer medium into which revelation was poured to be contained and carried or spilled and
lost. Time was the neutral alembic whose historical contents
were viscous substance—changing forms, altering causalities, partial and incomplete readings and judgments. It
became absolute history and transfigured time, when revelation effected the divine connection to the world.

It was possible, indeed mandatory, for Franz Rosenzweig
(near-convert to Christianity and near-apostate of Israel) to
devise a dialectic which initially regarded Judaism as beside
the point to Christianity, ineffectual and remnant, while
Christianity pressed the world forward to belief; and sub-

sequently, after his reversion to Judaism and lifting up of its teaching, to determine that precisely what made Judaism ineffectual in its first condition was now its genius and power, that it stood to the side of the world's history insofar as history is becoming toward God, but stood at its center insofar as Israel is constituted by God's revelation. The Christian presses forward through history toward the Kingdom, while for the Jew the Kingdom is always literally gathered in its midst, eternity prefigured in every speech-arrangement of the Jew's conversation with God.

Rosenzweig's theory has an elegance, indeed profundity, as a document of historical theology, an interpretation of Jewish pastness through the swamps of German idealist historicism, but can it sustain us beyond the *tremendum?* It would work had there been no caesura. If the Jews of our day had come up to these days without holocaust, but buffeted nonetheless by the strenuous contention of Johannine visionaries like Rosenstock-Huessy, Hans Erenburg, Viktor von Weizacker, and others within the Patmos Circle, or inspirited by Schelling's *Philosophy of Revelation* to dream the coming Kingdom of the undogmatic Holy Spirit, it would be no surprise that in their ambition to join up with history—active and militant conspirators of the Holy Spirit—they would be moved not toward Judaism but toward Johannine Christianity or into the humane socialism where Gustav Landauer, Walter Benjamin, Ernst Bloch, T. H. Adorno, and others found their arcane secular divinities.

It is hard to deny the temptation of history, particularly if all along one has been raised up to see the human *scenum* as the theater of meaningful action and event. Judaism, however, had for centuries located the sphere of its proper life to the side of history, not beyond it where it could not be touched nor where its unfolding energies could not be surveyed, but to the side, regarding it neither with disdain nor with envy, but with endless curiosity, as the enterprise of the

madness of the Gentiles, who revised their skins according
to the moultings of ideology and surprise, endlessly raising
up the offerings of their diversity to God for blessing or
pressing back the borders of darkness to avail the light its
dominion, but always tugging against time to relieve its
constriction and importuning salvation for its return. The
Jews have never been able to do this. Even though we now
regard Jewish history through Scholem's spectacles as one
by no means univocal, its counter-history, with all its an-
tinomianism and dissent, is still directed toward an acceler-
ation of the Kingdom's advent, not a denial that the Kingdom will come. Its mystical devices and practice still as-
sumed the nomenclature of historical Judaism as its form,
whether the traditional contents were emptied by alterna-
tive interpretation or filled with different liturgical language. There is no question in my view that the history of
Jewish religion is a history of a people that defines itself by
disciplines which either deny or more generally ignore the
interests, objections, claims, *realia* of the historical plural-
ity. Until recent decades, Judaism was, as Rosenzweig described it, ahistorical—not against history, but to its side,
not unmoved by its spectacle as human *passio*, but disen-
gaged from it as a spectacle of human ambition. Hence, it
was possible for Levi Yitzkhak of Berditchev to petition God,
during the Napoleonic wars, to have compassion upon the
Gentiles and to save them, even if God did not yet choose to
redeem the Jews.

But is this possible now? Clearly Rosenzweig and Buber
are mistaken in their constructed assumption that the
Jewish people—outside history as people or outside the welter of the historical in their ontological encounters of I and
Thou—has no history that is properly historical. The unreal-
ity of such history, or at worst a miscasting of the nature of
the historical as having its being in other than action and
nature (not excluding the nature and action of God, but no

less refusing to exclude nature and action, the exterior and the interior source of human growth as the grounds of the historical), is a denial of the temporality of Jewish history. But the Jew today is not the same Jew as the Jew of yesterday or the Jew at Sinai. The Jew has a history even it it is an extraordinary history. Historians who have no admitted need of a religious hypothesis are quite satisfied to deal with the Jew as an exemplum of the extraordinary, meaning by that little more than an exaggeration of conditions of biological disposition and enacted movement that constitute the freedom of any historical agent. The need to take the Jew out of history—a need felt throughout the tradition whether in its lachrymose expression as the special people of divine *passio* or its contemporary insistence upon the people as the agency of its self-transformation—arises from the insistent belief—a belief prior to all thought—that the people's origins are neither natural (that is, following from the forces of nature and life) nor human (that is, following from intelligence, imagination, and will). The people, the article of faith reads, is convoked by God and covenanted to him, certain fidelities being exchanged, certain marks of loyalty transacted as proof that the revelational relation has been established. Henceforth, though the people move through the medium of history, they are outside it—to be sure, tempted by the historical to will and project as would any other historical agent, but continuously reminded by the reassertion of revelation that its sole agency is God, that God is its king, ruler, authority. In such a view, there are only two historical modalities: faithful imitation of the ahistorical and unfaithful refusal of the ahistorical. The one is guarantor of peace and benefaction, the other of chastisement and punishment.

At the root of such doctrine—and it was, finally, the Rosenzweigian articulation of a traditional viewpoint—is the notion that the ahistorical Jewish people is a people that does not grow. The people's task is to listen in the silence that fulfills speech, in the patience that consummates prayer, for the rustle of the gathering Kingdom. The only movement is in eternity—eternity invading and transforming time. The only agent is the divine expansion, the self of God becoming toward a created being that stays put. For Rosenzweig the being of community is fulfilled in Israel, for Israel has all the being it requires for eternal life. It is, to be sure, created being and therefore a minuscule before the immensity of God's being, but it is fully delineated being which symbolizes the whole that becomes in God. Otherwise put, God's relation to the world and man is internal, since the world and man are portions of the divine objectification (that God might see and behold himself), and God grows as the world ages and man matures; the world for its part has no portion in God, neither changing its process nor altering its principle; man, for all his incessant acting, is already instructed by Israel that its way is eternal, its teaching eternal, God is in its midst in the fullness of its created being. God does not need man, but God grows through him. Man needs God, but does not grow at all. One must conclude that the form of the Jewish people is perfect created being, finite because created, temporal in that its end is always future, limited in that its space is conditional, but still perfected within eternity. Man's being is finished before God; God becomes toward the being of creation.

In effect the ahistorical Israel has no portion in growth. The Kingdom grows but its being is stasis and attention. God grows toward it in love, but Israel waits as an embarrassed lover, undeserving but endowed, contracted into the single mystery that it has become the beloved of God.

Quite a mystery, but somehow unaffecting, for a critical ingredient of the human complexity has disappeared, that of human freedom and human caprice. Or not quite, Rosenzweig would reply, for the Jew by circumcision is only instinctually Jewish, ordered in blood, but not in choice.

Freedom is to make the choice already necessary in blood, to confirm in the commandments what is already commanded to the blood. The last freedom of the Jewish person is to hear revelation. From the hearing of revelation and the acknowledgment that it is in fact heard as revelation, there is no longer freedom, for time disappears into eternity, self into community, active speech into the silence that awaits the renewal of the word, history into redemption.

Rosenzweig overstated the case. It is always the matter that theologians come to save others having first saved their own faith, wringing from their own unease a respite which conviction and hope move them to transmit to others as teaching. There is never final theology. It is always a theology of defensible structure, but the saving structure of one age is another's Tower of Babel, to be destroyed and replaced as the dreams of the creature and his intimacy with or estrangement from God are scrutinized and demolished. I find this no reason to despair of theological discourse, no reason to dismiss its findings. No different than other human disciplines that would wish to encompass all, theology is the highest inquiry and for that reason the most frail and tender, most given to pretentiousness and so desperately in need of modesty. Rosenzweig did save himself, but I question whether he has saved us. But then salvation is not the gift of theology, but the gift of God. The only thing theology achieves is that we might better understand how our salvation comes to pass, in what medium it is offered, through which human resource it is received. Jews contend, I believe disingenuously, that salvation has no portion in its imagination, that in doing the service of God, obeying *mizvot*, studying Torah, doing works of mercy to their fellow man they are doing what God requires of them that they be Jews. The circle closes upon them, God's will taken to themselves as their own, returning to God only the ontology of acts. There is no salvation in this, if by salvation is meant their being ransomed from sin or corruption (since sin and corruption are merely the correlative of not doing the commandments and its works) or restored to peace and self-harmony (since peace and harmony are within the Law, not attributes or rewards external to it) or the offer of eternal life in resurrection (since eternal life is given with the Law, death being no curse but eased fulfillment). Not salvation, but redemption is Jewish. There is an estate outside the Law which is the binding up and healing, not of persons, but of peoples. Redemption is not for the single man nor even for the single Jew, but for the Jewish people, the House of Israel. It is here that one returns to the eternal structure of the Jewish people.

The formulation that I would offer out of the thicket of this circumlocution is this: the individual Jew has no eternity, for he has no "midst"; the Jewish people has no temporality for it is always "in the midst." Less gnomically put, what I am struggling to identify is a proper distinction between the historicity of the individual and the eternity of the people, the fortuity of individual becoming and the necessity of the people, the endless variety and growth of the individual and the holy being of the people: theologically formulated, the individual is the work of creation, the people is the auditor of revelation. Adam is the stem of the race, but Israel is the stem of mankind.

V

The implication of this is in one respect clear. I have promised only to cross the abyss. I have not promised to explain it. I would not dare. What I have insisted from the very beginning until now is that the abyss consummated and torn out of the earth is now like the witness of a dead volcano, terrifying in its aspect but silent, monstrous in its gaping, raw in its entrails, visible reminder of fire and magma, but now quiet, immovable presence, yawning over the lives

of man. We may climb to its rim to examine its forbidding
ugliness but what we carry away is not the knowledge of its
being, but a memory of its being. What we preserve for ourselves and our generations is a symbol that narrates in the
mere mention a scarifying moment when it was active and
erupted. The *tremendum* is such a human volcano. There is
no portion of the human earth that is not burned; there is no
portion of the human earth that does not need redemption in
order that growth be renewed.

Earlier in this discussion I expressed a provisional pessimism. I spoke darkly in the language of history about the
Jewish people taking up the arms of history to come before
it. For those who caught my gloom, it may well have
sounded like the trope of one who stood outside not only the
Jewish State but also *propter hoc* outside the Jewish people.
Not at all. In fact, at this juncture, quite the contrary. Outside the Jewish State, any state for that matter, but never
outside the Jewish people. Indeed, it is precisely because the
Jewish people constitutes the eternal speaking of revelation
to the Jew of history, the turn of that people into the winds
of history, its taking up of the arms of the nations, is a turning of its guardianship of the word toward the nations,
rather than its traditional posture as merely concerned ob-
server. The being of the Jewish people is always behind the
becoming of the nations, its reformulation as State coming
at a moment when the states of the nations are weary and
declining, but this is the way of Being—imponderable slowness, because its renewals and conservations are outside life
and death, but always changes rung on eternal scales. The
way over the abyss that carries the Jewish people from exile
to renewal, from dispersion to center, from dissimulation to
exertion has now no visible meaning or import except to us
and not even to us, for not even we, as persons within the
Jewish people know anything but the signs and portents of
the being of the Jewish people. The being of such Being is

partitive and distinctive, sharing and participation, but without the perspective of the whole of Being. We are that Being, the Jewish people, but the perspective that makes it significant is God's and the meaning of God's self-narration is known only when it is done and past or else completed in the last minute of redemption.